DEATH

GRIEF

&

STARTING

AGAIN

This is the best book of its kind for all of us – now or in the future – that provides sensible, real life, information as if talking with a trusted friend who has lived and travelled this journey.

~Georgina Barraclough, Registered Nurse, Palliative Care/Complex Care/Rehabilitation

Death, Grief, and Starting Again is the author's story about loss, grief, the mystery of death, of ritual and practical necessities. Written in a conversational manner, it is told with warmth and compassion, preparing the reader for a profound experience that will inevitably affect us all.

~Maudie Palmer, AO

All of us must, at some time in our lives, endure grief. Who better than Diana to prepare us for this journey as she takes us through her grief and the lessons she has learned. But this book is more than that, it's a compendium to delve into when you need to know what to do next. And it's a comfort to know that whatever grief you are going through, others have gone before.

~Bruce Trethowan, Architect

Death, Grief, and Starting Again by Diana Morgan is beautifully written, funny at times and sad, as well as intensely personal. It is a practical guide to considering all aspects of aging and death with some very useful contacts at the end. I recommend it.

~Sue Matthies

One day we will face the death of a loved one. So why do we not prepare, even when we know that day is close? This is the book Diana Morgan hoped someone had already written when she faced her husband's death and its aftermath. As nobody had written the book she needed, she wrote it herself: a guide through the unfamiliar world of illness, death and grief – and starting life again. This is a practical, kind, and often humorous book, full of invaluable and interesting information. Diana takes our hand through a journey of preparation, as death forces us to think new thoughts and face new situations, from dealing with our grief and our family, to dealing with the government and bureaucracy.

And, despite its subject, it's really a book about life, and getting on with life.

~Vicki Steggal, Historian and writer

Published in Australia by
Cheverell Publishing
dianamarymorgan@protonmail.com

First published in Australia 2022
Copyright © Diana Morgan 2022

All rights reserved. No part of this publication may be reproduced, stored in a retrieval system, or transmitted, in any form or by any means without the prior written permission of the publisher, nor be otherwise circulated in any form of binding or cover other than that in which it is published and without a similar condition being imposed on the subsequent purchaser.

National Library of Australia Cataloguing in Publication entry

 A catalogue record for this book is available from the National Library of Australia

ISBN: 978-0-6454384-0-6 (paperback)
ISBN: 978-0-6454384-1-3 (hardback)
ISBN: 978-0-6454384-3-7 (epub)

Book designed by Sophie White

Printed by Ingram Spark

All care has been taken in the preparation of the information herein, but no responsibility can be accepted by the publisher or author for any damages resulting from the misinterpretation of this work. All contact details given in this book were current at the time of publication, but are subject to change.

This book is a general guide to difficulties you may face. Professionals should be consulted for individual problems. The author and publisher shall not be responsible for any person with regard to any loss or damage caused directly or indirectly by the information in this book.

Death, Grief & Starting Again

*Preparing for and dealing
with the aftermath of death*

DIANA MORGAN

*To Louisa and Rodney,
and John, Claire and Helena,
your support and advice is more
valuable to me than I can say.*

*And in memory of
Nigel, Henrietta, and Rollo.*

I include various websites in this book. Many of these describe local services, which I have been able to check. However, websites change so fast, and many are so localised that they are an indication only of what you will find helpful near you. I have included some overseas sites because of their interest.

CONTENTS

Foreword   11

Introduction   13

1   What happened to me   15
2   Planning for the future while still healthy   29
3   Thinking ahead – making sure your life is in order   37
4   Dealing with illness and planning end-of-life care   71
5   Dealing with the actual death   85
6   After a funeral – clearing up   111
7   Facing a new life   123
8   Fantastic facts, strange statistics, different traditions, and new ways of disposing of the dead and memorialising   149
9   Other people's stories   167

Acknowledgments   181

Useful resources   183

About the Author   191

FOREWORD

This book is intended to be a guide for the distressed, and a friend to the grieving, the confused and the bereaved. I hope it will be a companion for those who need to put a new and different life together.

Diana Morgan's *Book, Death, Grief, and Starting Again*, is about caring, dying, death and grief and then dealing with the bureaucratic aftermath as a surviving relative. At the outset, it deals with her personal journey after the death of Nigel, her much loved husband. She generously shares her experiences with everyone who will have to face similar challenges at some stage in their life.

Many of the matters she raises in her book are likely to await each of us, in one way or another. We know that to be true, but understandably we often take flight from the realities that face us. Here is a well-researched, readable, and compassionate book, the purpose of which is to help face these things and thereby overcome the anxieties that may lie ahead of us at some stage in the ageing process.

On a personal note, I know a little of Diana's journey and am also aware that there are helpful publications on particular topics also covered here, but a work covering the range of issues under one cover does not seem to be available in Australia, making it all the more valuable.

The book serves as a warning, though its aim is not to frighten but to empower the reader. Thus, instead of suddenly having to face a series of unfamiliar, confusing and painful events, we can all be better prepared by facing facts in advance and being better prepared in order to make life easier for ourselves and those around us.

We should read, absorb, understand, and so be prepared for whatever the future holds.

~Dr Peter Hollingworth, AC OBE

INTRODUCTION

You might say that most of us are *amateurs* at dealing with the disasters that befall us. The death of a loved one is one of the most common of all shared experiences and yet one of the least discussed. I wish I had known what to expect when it happened to me. I had no guidelines on living through it or putting together a new life afterwards. If this happens to you – you are not alone.

When I mentioned to a publisher friend that there were no books about this uncharted part of our lives, she said, "Write it."

So I have.

I have written the book I would have liked to have read at the time. It would have helped.

> You will need this book long before you *think* you need it!

A book cannot be all things to all people – one cannot deal with all the forms of loss it is possible to suffer. Nor is it possible to give you all the information you may need or in the depth you may need it. But I hope this book will give you some ideas about what is helpful to know, either for yourself or to help elderly parents understand what is necessary to think about and what help can be found. All the professionals I interviewed felt a book like this was needed so their patients would be more informed about the decisions, possibilities and alternatives that are available.

The information has clear headings so you can quickly find what you need. I have written about making sure your life is in order, about living with a sick person, what needs to be done when someone dies, coping with the aftermath of death, and what I found helpful in finding a new and, yes, happy path for myself.

There are many stories – mine and other people's – because it can be helpful to know how others coped. I hope your own path may become clearer as you read, so that you will be able to consider what is required and, most importantly, to do it on your own.

I hope this book will be of help. Your life will be different from mine, and you may need different solutions to the ones that helped me. I do wish you luck. Life mostly works out, I have found. But the older I get the less I am confident I will ever find all the answers.

You will find you can cope. You will become a fully-fledged member of:

'The OK Club, The Survivors'. Membership is free... and easy:

'How are you?'

'I'm... *OK.'*

It will take a lot of effort and a lot of time to work through to another, hopefully rewarding life. But it will happen. I was lucky that I lost a kind, funny husband who I miss rather than someone who I did not love and did not miss. But I now know that missing and mourning is a long, hard path with no end.

CHAPTER ONE

What happened to me

I learned that courage is not the absence of fear, but the triumph over it. The brave man is not he who does not feel afraid, but he who conquers that fear.

~Nelson Mandela

I had not intended to write about myself when I began this book, but it can be comforting to hear someone else's story, to know you are not alone, that someone else has been where you are finding it terrifying to tread.

My husband, Nigel, was diagnosed with terminal cancer. Six to seven months they said. No hope. In fact, he lived three and a half years after the initial diagnosis. It was dreadful to watch him slowly die. But don't pity me. I would not have missed a day of it – I had the luxury (and the agony) of being able to say a quiet goodbye and knowing that he knew I loved him and supported him every step of the way. Myself, I feel that the shock of a sudden bereavement – a heart attack, a car crash – must be much harder to bear.

Nigel was visiting London from Australia when we met. It was the swinging sixties. The first time I went out with him, he, my sister and a friend had dinner at an Elizabethan Banqueting Hall. There were loud songs, benches and wenches. I remember that in terror I had slid up the bench closer and closer to Nigel to avoid the lady next to me who kept cooing and squeezing my knee (lesbianism, then, was a distant, ancient, rather Greek, rumour). Nigel naturally assumed it was his conversation, his wit, his sex appeal and his charm that were irresistible. I was too shy, perhaps clever, ever to tell him why.

The next time I went out with him, it was just the two of us in a quiet restaurant and it was very, very nice. And I found that his wit, his conversation, his sex appeal and his charm really *were* irresistible! He listened and he laughed. We had so many shared interests. We were married in a tiny church in rural England, then drove straight from the reception to the airport and off to the other side of the world – everyone was sad I was leaving. I do not think I had understood the finality of what I did. For me or my family.

Our marriage was deeply companionable. Nigel did not just live life – he *celebrated* it. His idea of a perfect holiday was two museums a day. Mine might have been nearer one. He might have wished I had a few less interests but when he died, I was left feeling that I had been extraordinarily lucky. Your partner may die but the memories of the love, the battles, the births, the travels, the excitements as life unfurled underneath us, do not. Far from feeling alone I felt I had been left with great richness. In all the forty-seven years of our marriage I cannot remember him ever saying a word to me in anger, though I am sure I must have, on occasion, aggravated him beyond measure.

And then, the clouds came.

He told me quietly. I put my arms round him, and we stood, silent, grieving. Then: "I am glad you are sorry," he said.

The cancer was rare and strange, and we had the interesting experience of being asked if we would mind being treated in a teaching hospital.

"If they can learn from me and I can save anyone else I shall be glad," he said.

He was prodded and poked by successions of trainee doctors, plainly book-learned but visibly nervous at confronting a real, live, but terminally ill, friendly, and oh-so-vital patient.

Nigel did not want anyone beyond the family to know he was ill. Everyone handles illness differently, but he wanted to live as normal a life for as long as he could. It was very stressful for all of us to keep an outward veneer of normalcy. I felt I was living on a volcano as I tried to keep the cap on the boiling emotions inside.

I am sure it would have given him comfort to have talked about his situation, but he only referred to the future three times: would I remarry? No, I said. His shoulders slumped in relief, but no comment. Then: do remember to change over the car next year (I didn't). And perhaps because he and we had fought so long for his health, he asked for the great, loud Battle Hymn of the Republic to be sung at his funeral.

A joyful last family holiday

Nigel decided that we should go, as a family, on a holiday together, to give us all one last, glorious, shared memory. Our children had a wide age range. They had all had jobs interstate or overseas and it seemed a long time since we had been able to sit down and really catch up with each other. He chose to take us all on a cruise.

We knew we were all saying goodbye. From the first moment when we had to clamber over huge, snooze-eyed seals lazing on the steps that led down to the dingy, to the comfortable cabins (we had chosen a smallish ship but which was large enough to have a first aid nurse aboard in case we needed one) we knew this was going to be a holiday with a difference. The gentle islands we sailed amongst were the most comforting counterpoint to the emotions that swirled within us all. A daughter refused wine at dinner. Was this the longed-for pregnancy...

at last? There were lectures each night. If Nigel did not want to join an expedition he could remain on board and the rest could report the breathlessness of the day ashore. The memories of that time are powerful and strong.

We returned. The cancer was in remission, seemingly gone.

Extraordinarily, this was as shocking an adjustment for both of us – that life could go back to normal – as the original diagnosis had been dreadful; the end of life as we knew it.

Sadly, after a few months the cancer came back. For a further three years we faced a rollercoaster of hopes raised and hopes dashed. We made our way through cures working, cures ineffective, tried-and-true drugs, and the experimental 'it's-worth-a-try' kind.

Sickness

Friends did not understand if we left a party early or, having accepted, did not appear. We left a funeral halfway though. Nigel needed to leave, so leave we did. The whole gathering, seemingly, turned to look. Those who did not know us showed disgust at our rudeness; people who did know our story looked anguished, knowing we would not do such a thing unless it was absolutely necessary.

Slowly, Nigel began to look sicker. When his, you might say, *delicious* roundness gave way to a certain gauntness, he was congratulated on his weight-loss. There were many kindnesses but some friends could not cope, did not comment, faded away. Embarrassment? Sadness? There were surprises.

When Nigel was told more invasive treatments would prolong his life by only a few months he recorded his wish that he did not want to receive further medical intervention. He did not discuss this with me. I respected his decision more than I can ever say and hope, in my turn, to choose as dignified an exit. I have only slowly realised how much the approach he took helped *me*. The *grace* you might say, of his decision took much of the fierce regret, the choices, the grief from me.

He chose to have no further intervention. It was what he wanted. He did not want me to fight for any other course, treatments, medications. I had to accept this was his preferred option, his chosen path.

Nigel – thank you.

Upon his return from hospital, we were told he had three weeks to live. There was nothing more they could do, they said, but he was well enough to come home for a few days.

We remember little of that morning except for the tension at the hospital as we waited with him in a wheelchair until he was given the all-clear to depart. He was so thrilled to be coming home that he wanted to leave as quickly as possible. It was the morning rush – the nurses were busy, and we were allowed to leave without the formal checkout procedure. I had not been aware this is usually several pages of tick-the-boxes of information and instructions: Nigel had previously completed these forms himself.

Goodness knows how, but the hospital let us leave without his medications.

We had hired a hospital bed and commode. The downstairs study was ready to welcome him home as he would not have managed the stairs. Visiting him tucked up neatly in hospital we had not realised how much his condition had deteriorated. He had terrible oedema (fluid retention), he could not walk or stand. My daughter Henrietta was with me, but he was too heavy for us to manage on our own.

> Learn from me: we should not have been allowed to take him home unless we had had nursing help in place. His doctors may not have understood how far his physical condition had deteriorated in the weeks he had been in hospital, but his nurses would have known. The hospital should have warned us, made sure we understood. We were not told, and we did not *think*.

Over the course of the day, Nigel became progressively more distressed. We were slow to realise this was because his medications, which included large doses of painkillers, were wearing off. Unbelievably, no amount of hurried telephone calls could find anyone at the hospital who could give us the medicines or even issue new prescriptions for them. The hospital would have known, as we did not, how he would feel as the day wore on. His discomfort was dreadful to watch. It was a horrific situation. Our doctor was away at a conference, the palliative care nurses were booked to come the next day but that would not help us now.

In the early afternoon, realising we could not cope, Henrietta resorted to the internet and managed to get a nurse who could come immediately. An unlikely and ancient Mary Poppins arrived. She took charge of the situation and, casting many anxious glances at the patient, she described his symptoms over the phone to a locum in a long and detailed conversation. The phone was handed to me. The locum was kind. He prescribed a drug that would, he said, be of help. He could phone the script to the nearest chemist – could we collect it? Yes, of course we could. It was only afterwards that I found to my horror that the locum had used the generic name, a name I did not recognise, of a drug, a calmative, that I had been told not to give Nigel.

I had not been aware how expensive emergency nursing was. Even though this was many years ago the eight hours the nurse was with us cost $800. I believe it is even more expensive now. I say this because it was something we had not considered but should be borne in mind if a situation similar to ours ever happens to you. It had never crossed my mind that I would not be able to nurse him myself. You can see from the above narrative what a disaster it would have been on every level if I had been on my own, if my daughter had not been with me and, cooler and calmer, been of such inestimable help.

Henrietta drove off to collect the medication, and Nigel became more settled. The children came and we had an early supper gathered round his bed. We were all thrilled to be together again. Our grandson was too small to understand what was happening, and the dog tried to avoid being stepped on. There was much chaff, many jokes. There was a ceremonial uncorking of his favourite wine, a fussy arranging of the bendy straw in a glass (he could not actually face a sip, but he smiled at the fun of it all).

Our vicar was away, so I phoned an old friend, a priest. When, after university, our cohort had ambitiously aimed for the stars, he had taken a different path and began (at the bottom, we thought) with The Brotherhood of St Laurence, but Peter Hollingworth had achieved more than any of us. He came that evening not as our treasured friend but as the giver of comfort and understanding.

He put all ten fingers on Nigel's head. The prayer for the Comfort of the Soul and the prayer for the Dying – the words, powerfully honed by the centuries – rolled around our small study. I stood trembling from head to toe. As well as comforting my husband and me, the children were quite shocked at how consoling they found the ancient words. One of my sons is convinced the prayers said that night had given Nigel *permission* to die, that he accepted and understood; and that he knew we also understood and accepted that it was time. It is a comforting thought.

Perhaps no one can do anything kinder for a mortally ill fellow man who loved life and everything in it than to give him the confidence, the peace of mind, to leave it.

Peter – thank you.

We had a happy evening, made more poignant for all of us knowing it would be one of the last.

We did not know it would be *the* last.

Nigel became still more disturbed as the evening wore on. No one should ever have to go through the distress of that evening – watching helpless, someone in such pain. His groans still haunt us to this day. All because 'procedures' could not be followed by a hospital. If he had been a dog, I think they would have been kinder.

My daughter said that we had weeks ahead of us and that we needed strength to face the future and that we should go to bed. Nigel was quieter. The nurse said she would sit with him for the night, so just before midnight we went upstairs to get some sleep while we could. We were in deep gloom knowing that we could not cope with his needs, that the next day he would have to go back to the hospital, which would be really hard for him and for us to bear.

Death

At about 1.00 am the nurse came upstairs and found my daughter. I woke to see two anxious faces peering down at me. 'The nurse thinks Dad might have died.' She had heard a big sigh, she said, and thought he might have passed away. I had never seen a dead body before, but one look told me she was right. Nigel's eyes were still, staring with a strange luminosity. I had a sudden flashback, a strange stab of love – me in white, holding his hands, standing together in our tiny church 'In sickness and in health *until death do us part...*'. This was the PART bit. An extraordinary feeling swept over me. We had *done it!* We had loved and we had lived, and we had been together until the end.

I reached out my hand and gently closed his eyes. He was still warm.

Curiously the room, too, was warm. I had a strange feeling I had never experienced before. I felt that his spirit was still hovering, that the air was charged, vital. I was sure I felt something all about me fluttering, silent like birds, as comforting and as loving as ever. Was I listening to my own, racing, heart? Or could it have been him, having a last look around, perhaps a last look at *me? Imagination?* I wonder.

Might Nigel have still been in the room saying goodbye, perhaps, wanting to know we were sorry he was gone? It was such a powerful feeling that I still regret I did not talk aloud to it, whatever *it* was, or to his body as it lay there so still. But I stood, horrified, amazed, immovable. Perhaps, in retrospect, I really did talk to him on the level he was communicating with me.

We had to obtain a Locum Certificate, the nurse explained. She suggested a doctor, who came in the early hours of the morning. He spent an age testing for signs of life. He tapped, he took pulses, he stethoscoped, he peered. Could anyone who looked so very dead still be alive? I knew there was no spirit in the body I saw lying there, he was all too clearly gone.

The next morning everyone came back. We stood round his body gloomily sipping cups of coffee. I had to fight down a fair degree of hysteria. The hired bed had an inflatable mattress with an inbuilt mechanical movement intended to prevent bedsores. We could not turn it off, with the macabre result that the slight movement made it appear to us that he was still alive and still moving.

I had no idea what to do. I floundered. One of my son's had been at school with a boy whose father owned a funeral company. He rang to ask what we should do. Though distant, he said he could help, he would arrive mid-morning. The children felt strongly that Nigel should be sent off looking his usual elegant self. They selected his favourite suit, they busied themselves choosing a handkerchief for his pocket, a cigar and a box of matches (he had always ransacked every drawer in the house looking for matches). Small gestures of caring such as these are very comforting for us all to think back on.

The funeral director arrived mid-morning. He came with a very smart body-bag with a zip down the centre. We stood by while, making sure that my husband's nightshirt was decently smoothed, he eased his body into it. One last look at his dear face. Then he zipped it up.

We formed a guard of honour as he was wheeled out, as he had always wanted, out of his own house out of his own front door and out down the path to the gate.

I am still haunted by the sound of that zipper. Neighbours over the fence have an umbrella, perhaps a barbecue, that has a zippered cover. Whatever it is, remarkably often the sound of a zip floats from over the fence. And always I am right back in that room, appalled by the intensity and the regret of it all.

That morning at breakfast I had been ferociously hungry. I was stricken with guilt. Perhaps it was because of the shock of the night before, but how could I be hungry? How could I want to eat, how could I still love the feel of the sun on my arm, hear the laughter of our children when he was lying, dead, in the room next door and he could not?

I could not cry.

I wanted to weep. I needed to sob, to howl, to shriek. I *needed* to make noise as witness to my distress. I needed to keen. I needed to slump, moaning, in a chair red-eyed with a wet hankie clutched in my hand. Perhaps it was shock. A watcher would have thought I was frozen, stalwart, brave. Or worse – untouched, uncaring. Suddenly I was only half of what I had been before and nothing I knew could deal with this: The End. I mourned him in every other way possible. But... I could not cry.

I *can* cry. When lifting a two-year-old, heavy as concrete, to light a candle for the grandfather he never knew and he, thinking candles equals *birthday!* tried his hardest to blow it out; that alone-ness just before sunset when even the magpies seem to have tired of life; in a jolly crowd where I and only I know of the vast gulf, the chasm, the hole by my side. But sitting beside the shell of my beloved husband lying still. No. Strange.

I write this because I found myself unprepared for my own reaction. It took me a long time to realise that from the first moment when I had heard the diagnosis – the death sentence – I had begun to mourn. I had already built myself a fortress of many small mournings so that this last, big parting, this death, was almost an anti-climax after the turmoil that had come before. The initial diagnosis, all those X-rays that were not so good, the scans that were only so-so. The carefully crafted meals pushed aside, uneaten. The new medicines 'experimental but might be worth'... (*yes, yes, yes*)... that did not work. I had already mourned him and had been with him every step of the way in the years since the day he had been diagnosed as dying a slow, unstoppable death. My vigil was at its end. This actual death was almost easier to bear than the years of watching, being unable to help as he slipped helplessly through my fingers and out of my life.

I described these strange feelings to Janice Tully, a wonderful civil celebrant I met while researching this book. To my amazement and great comfort, she said this is a recognised phenomenon – *anticipatory grief*. She says it can happen, especially in divorce, that much of the sadness has been endured and has been worked though before the final inevitable event itself. All these years later a wave of acceptance and relief swept over me. Talking with the right person can be a better cure than anything else you can think of doing.

Bereavement is not simple. It is a complex maelstrom of feelings. And how much harder it must be if your departed is not missed or mourned. All those years of enduring dislike and perhaps hoping that one day this would occur: of remembering a person with feelings of cold distaste. My husband had been deeply loved but we were amazed that our overwhelming feeling when he died was of relief that he had nothing more to suffer, no further invasions of dignity. Most especially that he had not had to return, as he had dreaded, to the hospital. This curious elation carried us through the next two weeks.

Your experience will be different than mine, but you may face the same tumult of emotions. Do not feel guilty if you have such unexpected reactions; I am told this reaction to a death is normal.

Our funeral and wake

The reality is that you will grieve forever. You will not 'get over' the loss of a loved one; you will learn to live with it. You will heal and you will rebuild yourself around the loss you have suffered. You will be whole again but you will never be the same. Nor should you be the same nor would you want to.

~Elisabeth Kübler-Ross

Our service was warm and wonderful. Nigel had been a good, kind man, and had been much loved. He had many friends, so the church was packed. Everyone played their part to perfection. Lessons were read clearly, reminiscences were well chosen. He had requested The Battle Hymn of the Republic. When we reached *'He is trampling out the vintage where the grapes of wrath are stor'd...'* the whole church seemed to stamp in rhythm. Glorious. Cathartic.

We followed the coffin down the aisle and stood while it was slowly loaded into the hearse, and we watched as it was driven away to the crematorium, where we went the next day for a small family service. We then turned and went on to the wake held in the church hall.

I had dreaded the wake. I could not see the point of it. It was only afterwards that I understood the power of working though something you feel is unendurable. It gives you a strength you may not know you had. You need strong nerves, however. Perhaps people get nervous but some strange things were said. Someone approached with outstretched hand, smiled and said, 'Where *did* you get that *hat*?' I had worn a small, neat, black toque. I must have registered shock, and felt a steadying, comforting hand take my elbow. Someone had registered my distress, and I wish I could remember who that kind person was and thank them.

My memory of that day is fragmented. I remember a wall of kindness, empathy... a sharing. Seeing my children each surrounded by friends, quietly comforting. I wish I could remember more, but perhaps I am thankful I cannot. Never say to the bereaved: 'I know what you are feeling'. You cannot know the emotional mix of anyone else at such a moment.

In our case the evening of the funeral was sad and dreary. We were wrung out, exhausted. I had asked the funeral home to deliver the flowers from the casket to my house. The wreath lay down the centre of our table like a corpse while we ate takeaway pizzas sitting round it gloomy and glum.

The next night was different.

We had all been so glad that some of our far-flung relatives had cared enough to fly from around the world to be with us, that I did something I had never done before. To show them how much we appreciated their coming I asked a friend, a chef, to put on a dinner. It was the same price and far more suitable than a restaurant, which none of us would have wanted.

He came. He took over the kitchen. He had, seemingly, thousands of little plastic boxes with multi-coloured ingredients in them. He had a row of heat lights. He had a froth of pans. He rolled his eyes on finding I had no microwave. *Who*, I could hear him thinking, *does not have a microwave in this day and age?* I don't. My kitchen looked like a space lab.

It turned out to be the most brilliant evening. The chef was better than a cabaret. We all stood watching. Our small grandchild and the dog could snooze and be cuddled.

That evening taught me something very important.

We had a good dinner to be sure, but what we actually celebrated was the loving family web that had been woven by and around the man who was no longer with us. He, who was no longer the life and soul of the party was still the Guest of Honour. What we were, what the evening *was*, was what his life had been about. The love and the laughter and the memories tasted sweet as they flowed amongst us. It was a celebration of everything he had created and most valued and most loved. We talked and talked and 'Do you remember...', 'and that awful time when...'. We may have cried a little, but we certainly laughed a lot.

Such an evening is about people, not food. It is about laughter, remembrance; it is the interweaving of rueful jokes, recalled sorrows, memories, regrets, glorious gladnesses. A family gathering can be a simple matter of barbecue and rolls, it is the *getting together* of those closest that is remembered, and that is good.

CHAPTER TWO

Planning for the future while still healthy

I hold it true, whate're befall,
I feel it, when I sorrow most;
'Tis better to have loved and lost
Than never to have loved at all.

~Alfred Lord Tennyson

It is essential to plan for the end of life whilst you are well and healthy, long before such preparations appear to be remotely necessary.

Three things are essential: to put in place a Future Health Plan, then to ensure there is a mechanism for someone – or better two people – to manage your financial affairs if you are suddenly unable to do so and, thirdly, a Will. Nothing will give you more peace of mind than those three. The Powers of Attorney and Will section in this book explains these in more detail. It may all appear rather daunting but nothing will give you, and your family more peace of mind than to know these things have been thought of and are in place.

If you have had a very close partnership, you may not have thought of yourself as 'me' but rather as 'us' for a long time. Just accepting that a loss may be a possibility may help you accept that decisions need to be made, and it may give you a clearer idea of the possible future and hopefully make it feel less threatening.

Loss can be sudden: stillbirth, suicide. That dreaded knock on the door, the accident, the phone call in the early hours that changes everything forever. It can be the long, sad, slow goodbye of Alzheimer's or Parkinson's. Loss comes in many forms: the loss of your home, addiction. The gradual acceptance that a partnership is not the partnership once so joyfully entered into. People can mourn, deeply, the loss of a breast and all it means to them, to their lovers, to their children. But when I asked a friend who had had a double mastectomy if had she mourned, she looked at me as if I were mad. 'Oh no!' She was utterly thankful, she said, to have got rid the dread cancer and the slow, sure death it represented.

Great loss can be the loss of self-confidence after an accident, injury, a crime, job loss or retirement. The loss of dreams – infertility, poverty, the unfaithfulness of a partner, not finding a partner or the disillusion of an unhappy divorce. Family issues, financial anxiety or children leaving home. A beloved pet. For some people, the loss of a pet can be devastating; perhaps especially because it is likely to elicit less sympathy than the loss of a person. Some deeply mourn the loss of youth and beauty, the slow sadness of declining health, the loss of mobility or the necessity to live with the side effects of permanent medication.

> Whatever the loss it always comes in two parts: there is the loss itself and then there are the consequences of that loss, which can sometimes cause as much grief as the loss itself.

Death is the one thing we can all be certain of; the only thing we do not know is when, and how it will come to us. It can be sudden – an accident or a heart attack; or accompanied by the slow shadows of debility and forgetfulness. But if there is a framework in place it takes many worries away from dealing with future problems.

One of the major topics of this book comes next: making sure the affairs of you and your partner are in order, so that you can cope with loss when it occurs. It is sensible to think about the possible future. It is good to always have the basics of life in order. Sudden death or accident can happen at any age. Advances in medicine mean we live longer, but they also mean we are more likely to sink slowly into the mists of forgetfulness from which there is no return.

If you suspect that you or your loved one may have the beginnings of memory loss, make sure that you, or a person you trust, sorts out matters that cannot be executed without a signature – such as a Will. You need to plan ahead as a Will is legal only if it is signed by someone who is legally competent at the time of signing, and if the Will has been witnessed at the time of signing. It is salutary to remember that one in ten people over 65 and three in ten people over the age of 85 have some form of dementia, and once a person is diagnosed with this, it can be a difficult matter for them to legally sign a Will. In such cases you should seek professional advice. It may need two or more medical specialists to certify the testator is competent to make a Will. If a Will was signed by a person who might have been in the early stages of dementia at the time of signature, there could be room for a challenge.

Planning end-of-life care

It said that 75% of us have not had end-of-life discussions with our partner, but that 60% think we don't talk about death enough. About 70% of deaths are expected – people know that death is likely to be the endpoint of a chronic illness.

A survey of 1,500 physicians by the Royal Australian College of Physicians found that while the majority felt overwhelmingly that discussing end-of-life care was important, only 17% of them expressed confidence in knowing the end-of-life preferences of their patients. Of all deaths, over 80% currently take place away from home in a hospital or nursing home (another source says only 14–16% of people manage to die at home). Doctors may fear that discussing mortality will extinguish hope for a sick person, but many patients say they value honesty.

In discussions it seems sensible that death should be included as a probable endpoint. Some people facing death can feel they have had enough, but others try to hang on to see a child married or a grandchild born. One very frail person said that she had always thought she would prefer death if she became very sick, but when she came to that point, she could not bear not to see *what happened next.* But how long would you want to be sick? Perhaps you are scared of oblivion? The unknown? The Reverend Marilyn Hope, who has had a lifetime involved with palliative care and end-of-life situations at a large hospital, told me that most people are more frightened of the dying process than they are of death itself. Life, it seems to me, takes courage. Right the way along. And the end of life is no exception.

> *Death has this much to be said for it:*
> *You don't have to get out of bed for it.*
> *Wherever you happen to be*
> *They bring it to you – free.*
>
> ~Kingsley Amis

The appointment of a medical treatment decision maker (previously Medical Power of Attorney), A Future Care Plan, an Advanced Care Directive or a Power of Guardianship is essential to consider. These sound daunting, but they are helpful mechanisms to ensure that provision has been made so that someone, a family member or trusted advisor, is able to make decisions and deal with problems if a person is unable to do so for themselves. It is sensible to visit a solicitor and put in place whichever is best suited to your particular situation. 85% of Australians die after a chronic illness, not a sudden one. And 50% will at an end-stage be incapable of making their own decisions. Quite often the sick person finds their situation overwhelming and needs some help in making sense of the alternative paths available. The appointment of medical decision maker gives a chosen person, who signed the document, the power to decide on your behalf how you should be treated. If you already have the Medical Power of Attorney or some such document it will still stand, but as of March 2018 that document has been superseded by the medical treatment decision maker.

The holder has to present a signed copy of this power of attorney to the doctor, who may give them a choice of, say, three options for the patient's treatment and they will then decide what course of action is appropriate following the instructions that have been given. There is a small but important difference. The person appointed can make decisions *taking into consideration the beliefs or instructions* of the ill person. For instance, a Seventh Day Adventist or a Jehovah's Witness can instruct their appointee to refuse a blood transfusion even if the doctors believe it would save their life. Consult your GP perhaps on the wording and then make sure they have a certified copy on file so it can be quickly accessed if it is needed.

> Take care: It is a myth that more intervention is better in an end-of-life situation. Excessive care may prolong an agonising, inevitable ending.

Young people arrive in emergency mostly suffering from one complaint: drug/alcohol overdose, illness or trauma (car crash). Old people are likely to have a complex mix of complaints, which need to be quickly taken into account. If a person is taken to an emergency department and cannot communicate the staff are obliged to do their utmost to resuscitate them whatever their condition. If you have a Future Care Plan registered at local hospital and your GP has your preferences for end-of-life care, these can be instantly accessed electronically on entry. It is wise to include the person who holds these powers as well as the names of next-of-kin who can answer urgent questions if needed; this is good if the person who holds your Medical Power of Attorney cannot be contacted for any reason. The Care Plan will be drawn up with input from your GP, and your family should also be consulted. It is important to know that nothing you put in this is binding; you can change it at any time. Record in it if you prefer to die at home. The hospital will then begin treatment working down to a discharge plan if that is possible.

Although anyone can visit a patient in hospital, only the next-of-kin or the person who holds the Appointment of medical treatment decision maker or an Advanced Care Directive, which has been signed by the patient or a certified copy of it, has the right to make decisions about ongoing treatment. Important decisions will be discussed during family meetings, which are arranged by hospital staff. Medical staff will always do what is best for the patient, but they will not persist in giving treatment if they believe it is futile. Remember that in a highly-charged emotional moment a sympathetic doctor may have a more realistic view of what is best for a patient than the patient themself, their partner or their loving children.

Be aware that what people say about how they wish to be treated when they are well may change when death is near. One study found that just 43% of people who had written living Wills wanted the same treatment course two years later. It may be that life becomes precious when there is not much of it left. But few people say their priority is to live as long as possible; rather, their priority is to die free from pain and at peace. I hope I never have to face a slow, nasty end myself. It is a comfort to me that I have recorded this opinion[1].

Powers of Financial Attorney

When everyone is well and healthy it can be hard to accept that there may come a time when it may be necessary to have someone in place who has the authority to pay bills, and deal with financial matters on the behalf of another person. Powers of Attorney[2] are documents which enable you to nominate a particular person or persons to look after your financial, personal or medical affairs on a temporary basis (absence abroad, hospital) or long-term (ill health, cognitive impairment or in case of accident) These Powers ensures that a partner or family member has an account from which they can make necessary payments on your behalf when needed if you are not in a position or become unable to make decisions for yourself. If you have not nominated anyone, this power will devolve upon your next-of-kin (parent, partner, children) who will then have the power to decide matters on your behalf. If you feel that those closest

---

1 Read more at the Department of Health and Human Services, www.health.vic.gov.au
2 Free booklet available at www.publicadvocate.vic.gov.au/power-of-attorney

to you are not qualified to deal with your affairs, for example your children may live abroad or you may feel they are not responsible, you can appoint someone of your own choosing or choose a Public Trustee. It can be sensible to nominate more than one person so that decisions can be made jointly, as a safeguard or you can require that your bank statements go to another person, an accountant perhaps, or family member as a fail-safe so that all members of your family are confident your affairs are being dealt with sensibly.

If you are worried that you have greedy or unkind people around you, you can require that your bank statements are sent to another person, perhaps a solicitor, you trust.

Be thoughtful who you nominate to have these powers to assist you. Your closest and dearest may be the person least able to make a cool judgement in an emergency or indeed might be the person most likely to inherit your loot ☺ when you die. Someone slightly younger, more impartial might be sensible.

Power of Guardianship

A legal arrangement that enables you to appoint someone to be a guardian, who can make general health and lifestyle decisions on your behalf subject to any conditions laid out in the document.

You can obtain Will and Power of Attorney forms from the Post Office but it is sensible to obtain professional advice to make sure you understand what is appropriate for you. These documents need to be witnessed by two people 18 years or older, one of whom must be authorised to witness statutory declarations, such as a Justice of the Peace, legal practitioner, doctor, dentist, pharmacist, but not a relative or case worker.

Check the website of your local Justice department for a full list of people authorised to witness such a document, as it varies slightly from jurisdiction to jurisdiction.

Elder abuse

There is much concern at present that some elderly, especially if sick, highly medicated or suffering debility being vulnerable to pressures both from family and from outsiders who prey on them. There are many websites that offer advice on the subject should you be concerned.

My husband was a sensible and prudent man. But one day I overheard him being thanked effusively by the lady who came to help him with his paperwork. She had asked him for a quite considerable loan, he said, which he had given. I said quietly that it might be sensible to make a formal record of this agreement. He suddenly went pale and realised the position she had put him in.

The lady, big blue eyes brimming with honesty and sweetness, said the loan had only been for a very, very short time. Tax matters, she said, and she had been going to pay it back almost immediately. As far as I was concerned it was his money. He could do with it what he liked. But if anyone needed such a large amount of money suddenly, you can imagine that I was worried they might not find it easy to repay.

I felt this was someone taking advantage of a sick, tired man. Neither of us had at that time fully understood how much his ferocious cocktail of medications had blunted his usual common sense. A formal agreement was quickly drawn up and signed by them both, which was good. Blue eyes left his employ soon after, I am glad to say, which was even better.

> Important: there have been many cases reported recently, of strangers making friends with vulnerable people (joining elderly clubs, visiting nursing homes etc.,) charming them with a hard-luck story and then escorting them into their bank to withdraw money, which they promise to pay back but do not. Banks are legally obliged to pay out money if asked by a customer: they cannot refuse even if they are suspicious. If such a person's affairs are overseen by someone holding their Power of Attorney, there is at least a safeguard in place.

CHAPTER THREE

Thinking ahead – making sure your life is in order

Thinking ahead 1:
Wills and probate. Powers of Attorney and planning your own funeral

There was also enough light, Mma Ramotswe reflected, to see the world was not always a place of pain or loss, but a place where our simple human affairs – those matters that for all their pettiness still sometimes confounded us – were not insoluble and were not without the possibility of resolution.

~Alexander McCall Smith, *The Handsome Man's De Luxe Café*

PLANNING YOUR OWN FUNERAL

It can be sensible to leave instructions to your family about the sort of funeral of memorial service you would like. Readings, music, the eulogists. This can be helpful in avoiding family dissension during a very stressful time for them.

WILLS

A Will is a legal document that tells how the deceased has chosen to leave their assets. It is kind and thoughtful to make preparations for an orderly departure. You may think you have few assets and that a Will is not needed but dying without one makes your affairs hard to settle for those left behind. Joint assets are not distributed; for instance, the survivor becomes the sole owner of your shared home. If you have substantial assets, it is advisable to seek professional advice when making your Will. If there is likely to be dissention amongst the beneficiaries, or if provision needs to be made for the ongoing care of dependents or children, it is essential that a Will is drawn up professionally. The solicitor will keep the Will in safe custody, but remember to let family members know where it is. Families now often have a wide geographic spread. Laws can be different in each state and each country. If a deceased person has assets in two or more states and/or countries, the estate will generally have to deal with each jurisdiction. It is important to have professional advice if this applies to your particular estate.

A spouse has a duty to provide for their surviving partner. It is not sensible to leave a partner a life interest in the shared home, as the home may not be suitable in the long term, and the surviving partner may need to move to more suitable accommodation in time.

Before writing your Will, it is advisable to have a conversation with your family/beneficiaries to explain what you intend. Have this conversation earlier than you think is necessary rather than leave it until it is too late. The increase in divorce and remarriage and also longer lifespans has meant that nowadays there are often very complex family structures made up of more generations, more blended members, stepchildren, second families, for instance, than in previous times. If there are family members who are likely to argue, it is better to identify problems and try to find solutions before a Will is written than leave grounds for dispute.

It may be helpful to make a list of personal belongings you wish to leave to each child, for instance. You will want to maximise the amount of money you pass on, and the worst scenario is if you inadvertently give grounds for a family member to contest your Will. There is an increasing prevalence of people making claims for family provision against a relative's estate. Such fights can be expensive. No-one wins (except lawyers). Attention to small details can avoid much dissension after a death. If matters are hard to deal with now, they will be even harder when the person with the answers (you) is gone.

Many of us have responsibilities that we would like to be acknowledged at our passing. If a particular person is not receiving anything in your Will, put in a statement to say why. It maybe that you helped them buy a house many years ago, you might have invested in a business for them, or you might feel they would not use a lump sum appropriately (i.e., drugs, gambling).

It may be sensible to set up a testamentary trust for some dependants. This is useful for younger children or dependants who are incapable of managing money. A trust will protect their assets in case of divorce or bankruptcy and is tax advantageous.

Is anyone dependent on you, or has ever been dependent? They may have a claim. If provision has to be made for any person in particular, a good solicitor's advice is of immeasurable value. One in ten people, it is calculated, are carers who, after many years of caring and not being able to have a paid job, can be left on their own in a very poor way.

Do you have any personal debts? Liabilities? Hard-to-trace assets? Large items such as properties/businesses should be dealt with in your Will.

If your Will is extremely complex, the more chances there may be for someone to be able to challenge it. An experienced solicitor is likely to have seen every type of problem and will be able to give appropriate advice.

FARMING PROPERTY

Succession planning around farms, especially where certain family members work on the farm but others do not, needs more attention than just a division via a Will. Various claims may arise from someone who has contributed to the family farm in this way. Dealing with it in a Will may not be the best way of achieving a satisfactory outcome. It can be best to make arrangements for a division during the owner's lifetime. Constructive Trusts are a useful tool to set up arrangements so that the contribution of the person working on the land is recognised. They may have a claim given that they were promised that farmland, worked on it with little pay and relied on the promise of a larger share to their detriment.

> Remember the more complicated a Will, the more expensive it will be to administer.

WAYS TO SIMPLIFY YOUR WILL

Give gifts to people such as godchildren during your lifetime rather than in your Will. You can enjoy their thanks, and they can enjoy your generosity while they are young enough to benefit from it.

You do not want your family split by arguing over money. The Germans have a saying: *'Are you friends with your brothers and sisters still, or have your parents died yet?'* If you intend to leave the family home to one child, say, it can be simpler to stipulate that it is to be put on the market and bought back at market value and that the other sibling(s) retain their share of the sale price. You forfeit the transfer fee and auctioneers' costs, to be sure, but you save on solicitors' fees and have a demonstrably fair outcome.

BELONGINGS

It can be sensible to write a letter to be kept (by your solicitor) with your Will regarding the division of items of particular interest. This means that such objects need not be itemised in your Will. Write on the list that it is not to be included in the papers sent for probate. You may have items of value which your beneficiaries may wish to sell or share, in which case it can be sensible to suggest that they appoint a professional valuer or art consultant. These will charge a fee to estimate of values they might expect to receive at auction[3], which makes it easier to share fairly. All this should be discussed with your family.

Small items of sentimental value – keepsakes – may also be dealt with in a letter lodged with your solicitor along with your Will.

CHARITY

Many people leave money to a charity in their Will. Do not leave a percentage to a particular charity, as that charity then has the right to examine all your assets in order to check they have received the amount you stipulated, which can be difficult to manage. Remember that if you donate during your life, you will receive a tax benefit, which means you can give more. Your Estate does not get a tax benefit after your death. You can calculate a sum to be given to nominated charities and then put it in your Will as a percentage of your current assets – so that in case of disaster or jackpot your generosity does not threaten your financial world, but your wishes are clear to your executors.

PRACTICALITIES

Once probate of a Will is granted, anyone named in the Will or who would be entitled to a share of the estate if the deceased person had died intestate, or any creditor or guardian of a minor referred to in the Will, as well as any codicils, has the right to view the Will. Naming particular objects can be a good way to avoid disputes but be careful about putting assets of great value in a Will: 'I leave my Blue Period Picasso to my daughter Comeandgrabme Jones 15 Wanderin Street, Eltham' or 'Grandmother's diamonds and Aunt Etty's magnificent pearl necklace to my daughter Shyviolet Smith, Openfields Lane Abbotsford'. It is sensible not to specify the location of a valuable item (in case of burglars). Make a list of your valuables (perhaps two copies) detailing your intentions, have it signed and witnessed, and keep it with your Will. Lodge it with your solicitor so that it will avoid the public gaze.

---

3   info@bhfineart.com is one such company

FAMILY RELATIONSHIPS

Most families and marriages have some compromises whether large or small built into their fabric and there may be a matter left unresolved between a child and a parent. When family members visit, laugh with them about the wonderful and some of the awful stories that make up every family's life, but see if you can heal any breach, or bring a difficult situation such as a second wife/husband to an accommodation. Try to settle matters that might be the cause of powerful, lasting distress. Sadness after death is made harder if there is a legacy of dissent.

THREE STORIES ABOUT WHAT NO TO DO

Unkindness

A man asked his son to choose a painting from his very impressive collection. They had a happy day looking through the paintings and eventually the son, who was nervous – he knew his father – chose the painting he loved above all the others. He was then told, "Wrap it up and deliver it to your sister". The daughter took it. Every two months, it seemed, the father had told his children he had changed his Will. The brother and sister did not talk at the funeral nor in all the years thereafter. If only she had said, "brother, I will keep this for you and let us divide 50-50 whatever he does". But no. The father got exactly what he wanted – he spread further the unhappiness he had had all his life. Bad man.

Spiteful selfishness

A man's second wife was joyfully describing to a group of friends her latest wild extravagance. She had been left his entire estate for life, with it devolving upon her death to her husband's only beloved daughter. Her voice changed to a snarl. "I am going to see that she does not get a penny of it." Perhaps she saw the shock on my face; we haven't talked since. Silly man to be so thoughtless.

Sadness

A daughter nursed her mother for 20 years, unable to work or save. When the mother's Will was read it was found she had left her house, her only asset, to her son, leaving the daughter homeless. Thoughtless mother.

Actions like these do not just echo down the decades, they reverberate. Make sure you don't do anything like them.

And a fourth

I heard of someone who, when told that her husband, on life-support, could no longer be helped, delayed the switch-off for a day until she had moved his frequent flyer points into her name. Someone, she said, might as well enjoy them. The husband had travelled a lot and that asset would die when he died. She thought this was clever and funny. I thought it was clever, but I am not so sure about the funny!

AFTER DIVORCE

It is essential to know that divorce makes an existing Will invalid, and a subsequent marriage revokes an earlier Will. It is remarkable, apparently, how many people divorce, remarry but do not write new Wills. This could mean that children, past spouses, dependents etc., are unprovided for.

FLEXIBILITY

If there is likely to be a long time before the Will takes effect – say, if dementia seems a possibility; it may be appropriate to set up a trust, and write a non-binding letter of wishes addressed to the trustees. The non-binding letter can be updated if necessary, and allows the trustees to have a guide to the deceased person's wishes but gives them certain flexibility within the structure of the Will to take into account family circumstances which may not have been foreseen when the Will was written.

EXECUTORS

The executor is the person(s) named in the Will who will ensure the estate is distributed according to the wishes of the testator. Whether it is better to have one executor, or several executors depends on factors such as the complexity of the estate to be administered or perhaps the number and qualification of family members or friends who can fill the position. It may be helpful to choose more than one so that discussion and negotiation can take place if there is a difficulty. You need to discuss with the person(s) you select if they are willing to act as executor, and also agree on an appropriate fee set into the Will for performing the duties involved, if this is likely to take a lot of work.

Executors are required to apply for probate. They will close bank accounts, pay tax, funeral costs, retrieve nursing home bonds etc., organise the collection of the deceased's assets, pay outstanding debts and distribute the balance according to the deceased's will. These duties are generally expected to be completed within twelve months, though a house may take longer to empty, prepare for market, sell and settle. If the Will directs the executor to set up trusts which may continue for many years, the role of the executor will change to that of a trustee of these trust estates.

Executors who make mistakes can be held personally responsible. It may be sensible, if you are asked to be an executor of a complex estate to take out liability insurance: a policy that protects an individual executor against legal or financial claims resulting from their actions. Remember, probate can take six to twelve months to be granted, but insurance policies are annual, so make a note to keep up the payments. Solicitors have deed rooms where they will store such documents for you. Your solicitor can act as executor but may charge a substantial fee.

Executors can find themselves in a difficult position. One reputedly dysfunctional father asked his youngest daughter to be his sole executor. Her five siblings were irresponsible, flighty, or bi-polar. His daughter's job in IT was teaching machines to talk to people, and he felt she would be able to keep her brothers and sisters all talking to each other. Every year she had lunch with her father on the day before his birthday, kept notes of their conversation and sent them to all her siblings. This meant they were all assured she had their interests at heart and was caring. Clever father, sensible girl.

STATE TRUSTEES

If you have no one to appoint as an executor, you can appoint a trustee company or the state trustee to administer your estate. Understand that your family cannot remove a corporate trustee once one is appointed. The charges can be large, I understand, and are calculated as a percentage of the asset value, varying with the size of the estate.

A friend has chosen this option. Very bright and in her 80s – 'but I have to die sometime' – she told me she had been an only child and had no children of her own. She had twenty cousins, but they were all aged and distant, and she did not know any of their children. She had seen a friend's estate, which had had complicated family difficulties, dealt with very sympathetically by the state trustees. She said she had been impressed at how kindly they had dealt with her own enquiries. They had agreed that after her death they would arrange for the charity Caritas to come in and remove her books and clothes for sale in their op-shop, that they would auction her house and all her personal belongings and then divide her assets between the three charities named in her Will.

What I was left with, which I pass on to you, is the peace of mind it gives a person to know that they have left no problems behind them, that their life will be laid to rest and settled as they wish.

DYING INTESTATE – DYING WITHOUT A WILL

You may think you have little of value and that a Will is not necessary. But the little you have might mean a lot to someone else, and the intention of kindness can be as great a treasure as treasure itself. Properties can rise in value unexpectedly and you might win the lottery the week before you die!

A survey in the United Kingdom found that 30% of adults had never made a Will. If a person dies without a Will that person is described as *dying intestate* and their estate may take a great deal of work and also cost several times the amount to clear up compared an estate with a valid Will. The assets will be distributed to family members according to a formula set down by the law of intestacy, which may not reflect the intentions of the deceased. A distant cousin may inherit rather than a close, kind friend for instance. The estate is likely to be administered by a public office holder such as the state trustee who employs a team of genealogists to find relatives, however distant, who are legally able to inherit the estate. If no relatives are found after five years, the estate passes into the public purse. So make sure that everyone around you has a viable Will. To wind up an intestate estate, letters of administration have to be applied for, not probate.

The cost of dying without a Will depends on the jurisdiction and also how distantly related the person is and what needs to happen to show that they are next of kin. If it is relatively straightforward the costs may not be much more than for a grant of probate. If a genealogist is required, the costs can be much higher.

The laws governing intestacy differ from state to state, country to country. Three respected solicitors I have consulted have given me three slightly different versions of how they think the law is applied. Buy a Will kit from your local post office/newsagent *today* and *use it* if you have not written a Will. But be aware that in recent years a high proportion of do-it-yourself Wills have been challenged, which can result in expensive litigation as even the simplest estate may have complications you have not foreseen.[4] Take care.

DE FACTO PARTNERSHIPS

If, as my grandmother would say, you are in an irregular union, including a same-sex one, it may be as well to check your status. I have been assured that de facto relationships (after two years) have almost the same status as far as inheriting estates goes, as married partners, but I have heard several stories that suggest this is not always so. Take care.

---

[4] Martin Luther King, Prince, Jimi Hendrix, Amy Winehouse, and Brett Whitely died without valid Wills. In most of these cases, the disputes are still raging years after.

LEAVE CLEAR INSTRUCTIONS

Make a file labelled clearly 'Will' and 'Powers of Attorney' in big letters, perhaps in red, so that it can be found easily amongst your files. It is important to tell members of your family that you have done this, which documents are in it and where they can find it if it is needed.

Next step: Take two A4 envelopes.

ENVELOPE 1

This envelope is to be kept at home in your 'Will' file. Put the following essential information about yourself (and your partner) that might be lost or hard to find at the time of your death (or dementia) and write clearly on the outside what is in it, and the date any document was updated.

1. A certified copy of your medical treatment decision maker document. Tell family members that it is in this file or who has it so it can be accessed in an emergency.

2. Organ donation. If you have left instructions to donate organs upon your death, keep your donor's card here. Also list your blood group.

3. Funeral. If you have chosen a funeral company or have instructions for your funeral put them here or with your vicar or priest but put a note here to say where they are. Have you a pre-paid funeral? Record details if you have purchased a grave site. Your instructions are not legally binding; your family need not follow them, but it gives them some guidance as to your preferences.

4. You may like to keep a copy of your Will in this file. Solicitor's offices are closed at weekends if it is needed in a hurry (for organ donation for instance).

5. A list of any information you have lodged with your solicitor which may include your credit card and bank account details, your Will, Powers of Attorney. Never put such documents in a safety deposit box as this may be closed on the death of the owner

until probate has been granted... which is difficult to obtain if the necessary documents are not available!

6. Keys to your safety deposit box, PO box, or a note to say where you keep them. Also the password. You may want to give this information and the keys to two separate people so neither can access the box alone.

7. If you have written a letter detailing the disposal of your chattels say so here, but put the actual letter in the solicitor's envelope for safe keeping (so no family member can be tempted to suppress it if they disagree with the contents).

8. Names of any banks, professional advisors who may need to be contacted: solicitor and doctors especially, but also credit cards, bank, accountant, stockbroker and social worker.

9. Your current digital passwords. Passwords can be a nightmare. Think hard about how you can keep an up-to-date record of them so that if you are suddenly struck by confusion or are involved in an accident, essential sites can be accessed by someone you trust, but not by casual or hired help.

10. Professional colleagues, overseas friends, people who your family may not know but who you would like to be notified of your death (with email or phone numbers).

11. Optional extra. You may like to suggest to your family that you have a copy of their passports, funeral instructions, any relating correspondence, in this file. Of course, everyone will have such information on their own computer, but late at night, sudden phone call, child in a foreign place... you can quickly access information if needed[5].

ENVELOPE 2

The second envelope to be given to your solicitor or close, trusted friend should contain the following:

1. The Will (the solicitor may already have it).

---

[5] Sally Clarke's *How to Die Happy*, is a good check-list resource to have at hand; it is small, and you could fill it in and keep it in this file.

2. A letter detailing matters about the disposition of any valuables, paintings, jewellery, that you have not put in your Will.
3. A list of information such as safety deposit box, where it is, number of the box, access code, name of co-signatories etc., safe combination, PO box, hard to trace assets.

> Note: Information in points two and three should not be kept in your home file, just in case someone goes to it ('She always said *I* could have it') or tears up a letter ('She promised it to *me* not *her*').

These are small, thoughtful ways of avoiding dissention amongst your heirs if you think it is likely to occur. Your family, your assets and the law can change:

THE 5 DS: REVIEWING THE POWERS OF ATTORNEY AND WILLS

Decade: *perhaps every big 'O' birthday.*
Death: *of a close loved one may alter situation of the people around you.*
Divorce: *existing Wills, Powers of Attorney can be nullified. Check.*
Diagnosis: *if you are diagnosed with something life-changing.*
Decline: *when such documents become more relevant.*

INTERGENERATIONAL EXPECTATIONS

It is said that the present generation is the first to grow up poorer than its parents. It is faced with soaring house prices, student debt and part-time work. Earlier generations were faced with full-time work on pay so low it was impossible to save, parents whose lives had been wrecked/shadowed by The Depression/World War, and most of them would have given their eyeteeth to have the education available if they had been able to take out a student loan. How hardships change!

BOMAD (BANK OF MUM AND DAD)

It is natural to want to help the young acquire education or get their feet on the property ladder. In Australia there are no restrictions on the amount you can give family members, but laws can always change and can also be made retrospective. Countries vary. Currently in the United Kingdom, for instance, you can give away a lump sum of £3,000 each year. Cash sums of more than that are exempt from inheritance tax only if you survive for seven years after making the gift. Should you die within those seven years, the gifts are taxed at a tapered rate.

LOAN OR TRANSFER OF MONEY IN EXCHANGE FOR CARE

Be careful about the possible consequences of giving money to assist with buying a child's house which has a granny flat attached. It sounds sensible. You get observational support, they get loving babysitting. Take care. Get independent advice. Discuss with the wider family. If you come to an agreement, document and sign what you have done. Such decisions can affect your pension and tax, let alone family relationships. Difficulties can arise if, for instance, you need to go into a nursing home – whose is the asset? It cannot be sold separately, and you may be unable to raise enough money to sign a bond for a nursing home. And does it mean that other siblings do not get that share of your estate?[6]

If you wish to give money to a married child, you may like to consider a legal cohabitation document to ensure that any deposit you hand over is returned to you or stays with your child in the event of a marriage break-up. Or you could ensure the gift is part of a pre-nuptial agreement that the property will stay in the family if they divorce. You can set up a discretionary trust, the money from which can be accessed at certain ages or for certain purposes (deposit on a property or university fees, for example). Trusts are expensive to set up and run but can be a good idea especially in cases where there are large assets, and the young person may be unsupervised or flighty.

---

6 There are several good websites that deal with such difficulties, such as www.seniorsrights.org.au

It is important not to tie things up too thoroughly; life requirements are fluid. It is also important not to write provisions in the first flush of family discord, or indeed youthful rebellion!

A commonly imagined scenario is that a much-loved grandchild might eye Nonna's house and dream that his/her share of it might one day be enough to be a deposit on an apartment in the wonderful block being built just around the corner. Nonna might feel that after all the long years of caring for Nonno that she might just like to join her best friend on a *Cruise! Whee!* Nonna may have been careful with money all her life. She may have bought carefully, wasted little. The beloved grandchild born in a different era may feel the odds are stacked against him/her owning a house of his/her own. To Nonna (though she would never criticise) their internet shopping/cafe hopping lifestyle might seem wasteful. Should she have a chance for the first time in her life to try smashed avocado for brunch, perhaps.... to be treated, rested, stimulated, amused?

But take care. Aging people do not always accept that they may need to provide for themselves for a longer time than they expect, and they may not foresee the large costs that can be involved in end-of-life care.

An interesting new firm, Ageing by Design[7] has been formed by two experienced solicitors who have also had to navigate issues associated with ageing on behalf of their parents. The business provides comprehensive specialist advice about accommodation options and government services that are available as people age, as well as advice on all associated legal issues – Wills, Powers of Attorney, Appointment of Medical Treatment Decision Makers, Advance Care Plans, guardianship/administration applications, and all contracts and fee structures relevant to accommodation options. This last could be especially useful as I describe that such contracts can be most complex. They also provide an objective sounding board to enable the different viewpoints that are often present in any family to be heard in order to ensure the interests of the older person are properly looked after.

There is much to ponder.

---

7 ageingbydesign.com.au

Thinking ahead 2: Planning your digital after-life

PUT IN PLACE A DIGITAL ASSETS MANAGEMENT PLAN OR DIGITAL ESTATE INVENTORY

Usernames or passwords are now needed to access essential information about our lives, our bank accounts, personal data, photographs and the like. It may be sensible to appoint a computer-savvy family member to put in a system so that at least someone knows how to access your digital information in case of your death or incapacity, and most importantly who is able to keep the system up to date. Discuss with family members.

Create a system so that casual helpers or vexatious family members are not able to 'help' by accessing private and financial information. An easily accessed list of all websites/passwords could be highly dangerous if it ever fell into the wrong hands. But balance this against the problems that will be faced by those clearing up your estate if there is *not* one!

Consider your or your loved-one's digital afterlife, the digital legacy and how you or they want digital information to be dealt with. Remember that many online businesses store credit card data. It is important for all family members to make certain that passwords are written down, and *not changed* without family knowing so that help is available should the user become forgetful or unexpectedly unable to deal with essential matters. A friend told me that her husband (one of those wonderful, dependable 'leave it to me, darling' type men) clever and able, sat down at his computer one day and could not remember a thing. It can happen out of the blue.

Keep a list of up-to-date passwords. Ask your partner to do the same, and tell someone close to you where they are kept! Passwords are hard enough to remember at the best of times but can become problematical for anyone with lurking memory loss. It has been said that the average employee has 191 passwords. I have one that I use for a lot of non-important sites, then special ones for particular sites.

I find I frequently need to make up new passwords to access simple internet services. I mean to always add these to a list I keep, but...

There are apps that will store your various passwords, but a computer geek I know puts all his on a stick which he hangs on a hook on his dresser so his wife could find it if necessary. There are computer experts who are able to bypass some (but not all) programs.

The trend to fingerprint access for some digital devices is a further complication. The University of Michigan has created a silicone hand which can obtain fingerprints (from a house, office, car) and then make a silicone glove impressed with those fingerprints that can gain access (think safety deposit boxes, banks, airports, security areas – places which use biometric hand-print access) without the presence of the initiator. But would you relish visiting the funeral home with a wad of silicone to get the deceased's fingerprints? A case was reported where the police had done this in order to access a victim's mobile phone. Access using facial or iris recognition, which is becoming more popular, can also be problematic. I am told a photograph of the deceased will not work. I am told that a colour-photo wrapped around a hot water-bottle will not work either. Photographic ID needs to register the 3-D warmth of a whole face.

Digital technology is changing so fast that anything I write will be out-of-date before this book is published. There are several programs that deal with end-of-life problems but I have heard they can be less than satisfactory. Google has a program called Inactive Account Manager[8]. It claims that it allows users to decide how long data and photos are kept, and also to nominate others who can log-in but personally I found it difficult to use. Facebook has a memorialising facility so that it can remain accessible after a death.

There are many helpful websites that can provide up-to-date information.[9]

Hicks, Oakley, Chessel, Williams have a good digital register checklist you can download.[10]

---

8   https://support.google.com
9   www.awayforabit.com
10 www.hocw.com.au

You could also check out Dr Elaine Kasket's book on dealing with digital legacies.[11]

Thinking ahead 3: Money matters

Make sure you will be able to access funds for necessary expenses in an account that is not linked to your partner's. I have been advised (by a solicitor) that if your account is linked it is sensible not to inform your partner's bank of their death until you are certain you have access to sufficient funds to cover immediate costs.

Remember, the moment a bank is aware that someone has died, it will freeze their account until probate is granted. A bank will release funds if given an invoice from the funeral company for funeral costs and they will also release funds to cover probate fees and tax. All statutory payments, bills etc., and also Powers of Attorney will automatically stop on the death of the account holder.

A friend, suspecting my husband was ill, quietly advised me to make certain that in the event of his death, I would be able to survive financially in the immediate aftermath. I wish I had listened to her. It would have saved me from much anguish. Money affairs may take months to sort out and you will not be able to access money from a joint account until after probate has been granted (three months at the earliest).

My husband and I did not have a joint account. If you have a joint account, the surviving spouse can access funds upon the death of their partner. I had a linked account, and we had each operated our own accounts quite independently. I had the responsibility for certain expenditures while he dealt with others. I had not understood that while he was the primary cardholder, mine was the secondary linked card. It never struck me (or him) that I would have any difficulty sourcing money when he died, but I discovered that I had

---

[11] Kasket, Dr Elaine, *All the Ghosts in the Machine: Illusions of Immortality in the Digital Age*

no individual credit history (as everything had been in his name) so I had trouble proving I was good for the $$$.

My husband's assets were frozen at his death and would not be released until probate was granted. Suddenly, I could not access any money. I could not use my credit card or a cash machine. The tellers who used to smile as I neared now snarled as if I was a menace with a loaded gun trying to rob them! I had to borrow money from my children in order to eat. It took three weeks, an enraged son accompanying me *(the humiliation)* and making a terrible fuss to re-open a new account. I happen to be nervous about computer fraud and we had always preferred a very small overdraft facility. Insult was added to injury when I found I would be issued with a new bank account but only if I agreed to an overdraft several times the one I had had before. In one fell swoop my bank went from being a friendly organisation to an inhumane and uncaring enemy.

Losing a partner must happen to a great number of a bank's good, steady customers who are likely to remain good, steady customers until the day they die. Customers are unlikely to disappear into a cloud of smoke or even into cyberspace. It amazes me that banks have not instituted a system that acknowledges death is a possibility and if necessary, courteously bridge a common, and often unexpected and embarrassing gap until new arrangements can be put into place.

In a rage I visited all the main banks and enquired if they had available brochures for their clients with advice for such eventualities. One said yes but could not find it to show me. Another said yes, but we only give them out if people enquire – *it might scare our clients* (my italics, not his). My bank said no, they did not.

Glossy, friendly brochures full of advice about other services tumble out of every bank statement I receive. There is always a kindly, smiling, plainly ignorant old granny on the cover. I put them straight in the bin. They do not apply to me. I know better!

Make a list of the essentials that you will need money for over the year until you can expect probate to be granted.

It may be sensible, if you are able, to quietly open an extra, independent, account so that you can access funds in such an emergency. Try to ensure you have funds put aside so that you are able to manage.

These may include:

- Solicitor and accountant fees
- The likelihood of meeting outstanding costs for the person who has died: medical, hospital, funeral etc. Medical cover for yourself and doctors/medical costs likely for yourself
- Outgoings on your living place: rent? Mortgage payments? Body Corporate fees, and maintenance. Rates? Your living expenses: food, electricity and gas.
- Did your partner have responsibilities towards family members? Education or the like?
- Car insurance and car service. Petrol.

Thinking ahead 4: Donating organs or your body for medical research

There is a growing understanding that our body has a huge potential to be useful to others after our death. If you wish to donate your organs you have to opt in. Register your intention online and then sign the permission forms that you will be sent. Let those around you know that you want to do this. Organs will not be taken if someone has not given written permission and even if the patient has signed up to donate their organs, permission is always asked from the family (who often do not agree to it).[12]

Out of the Australian population of 25 million, in 2019 only 683 lives were transformed by donations from 548 deceased and 239 living

---

12   www.humanservices.gov.au

donors. A further 12,000 benefited from eye and tissue donations. The waiting list to receive an organ transplant usually numbers around 1,600. 12,000 receive dialysis treatment but are not suitable or cannot find a donor. Weep for those waiting who, unlike me, did not find a solution and had to watch someone die. Although 69% of people say they are willing to donate upon their death, far fewer actually register to do so. Many European countries, including England as of May 2020, are bringing in legislation so that when a person dies their organs can be retrieved if needed. If you do not wish for this to happen you have to take steps to opt out.

Under 1% of deaths take place in conditions where it is possible to collect a donation. There are two kinds of 'eligible' deaths when organs can be taken.

First: after *brain death* (such as a traumatic head injury). Such a person may be able to donate many organs because even though their brain is dead their heart continues to beat, and their organs remain viable for transport.

Second: *Cardio-circulatory* death after the donor's heart stops beating under controlled conditions in hospital. Fewer organs are available under such conditions. Brains and hearts have to be collected within 24 hours as they both deteriorate quickly, whereas skin (used for burns, scars) and corneas are not as time-sensitive and can be collected up to four days after death. A newspaper article (February 2020) describes a new machine, Ulysses, which will hopefully come on the market soon. It is compact enough to be carry-on luggage in an aircraft so that it can be quickly transported. The machine acts as a surrogate body – the heart is chilled and oxygenated saline fluid is pumped through 60 times a minute, mimicking the beating of a heart. This would give surgeons more time to match donors to patients. Interestingly, many brain donations to research organisations are made by people hoping that their brain problem can be researched, and a cure found for someone else, but there is a shortage, apparently, of *normal* brains which is necessary to study for comparison. If you gift your whole body for medical research or training, I understand that a payment is made to you that is equivalent to the funeral costs you would otherwise have borne. Neuroscience Research Australia (NeuRa) in Sydney hold about 600 brains in the hope that studying them may help find cures for some of the neurodegenerative diseases such as Alzheimer's or Parkinson's that result in distressingly slow deaths.

My personal experience explains why I am keen to explain this issue. Shortly after my husband died, I sat in the emergency section of a big hospital with my son's new, young wife. We had not known my son was ill when my husband was sick, or indeed when they had married. Flat, weak, pale he was floating in and out of consciousness before us. He was a week away from his sister donating a kidney to him (I had not been compatible) but he, we and the machines he was hooked up to all thought he was dying. We sat quiet as mice, willing the doctors not to stop their efforts even for a second. Whenever he came out of the clouds, he cracked a stupid joke. He said later he thought it might stop us worrying. We felt it had added to the terror. I can recall no clocks in our small cubicle, but he said he had never watched a second hand go round so slowly.

What surprised me was my reaction. When my husband was terminally ill, I had been philosophic, kind, consoling, taking comfort from 'In sickness and in health until death do us part'. I had accepted that this was the final part of the contract we had made when we married: to care for each other till one of us died. As I sat watching my son, I *raged* inside. I would gladly have given my life for his. I shrieked inside for more ancient gods, gods who whirled with mouths agape, gods with rebellion, rage and revenge in their hearts.

When a partner dies after a full and joyous life, well-loved and having, so to speak, sucked the juice out of life, one has to accept that it is part of an inevitable continuum. If a child is sick, it is an entirely different matter. It is awful to reflect that I am, perhaps only the second generation of parents who can confidently expect not to lose a child to sickness. Whatever gods the parents had prayed to over all those tens of thousands of years as they watched a child sicken, my good fortune was to live near a hospital staffed with good doctors. My son recovered. I am not so sure that I ever have!

John Surtees' (the racing driver) obituary recounted that when his son Henry was killed in a racing accident his wife persuaded him that Henry's organs should be donated for transplants, even though his instincts were to keep his body whole. The donated organs, his heart, valves, liver, kidneys and pancreas saved five lives, including that of a six-month-old baby.

Having seen both the despair and the joy associated with organ failure and donation, I find it is a most appealing thing to do, a small price to pay for life.

REGISTER AS A DONOR

If, like me, you know what it feels like to sit with a child who you think is dying, you will understand the joy of donating your body so that someone else may be saved. Burial customs which value the 'whole' body are traditions with their roots in earlier times. I am glad that medical science has given me options that were not once available.

Notification of your intention to donate has to be made by you, the donor, before death so that your wishes can be carried out immediately upon your death. If you donate organs, it makes no difference to the medical care you receive before your death. There are no costs involved for the donor. Organs are removed if needed, and your body is then taken to the funeral home and the funeral can proceed as usual. There is no visible sign that organs have been removed.

If you donate your *whole* body to science for research or training new doctors, it is embalmed, and the ashes are returned to your family perhaps a year later. In that case – hold a memorial service, not a funeral!

It took me two minutes on the internet to register my wish on an easy-to-use website[13]. There was a choice of which organs you wish to donate. I ticked the *all* box. Shortly after I received a letter asking me to sign and return a form to confirm my wishes. I then told my children what I had done so that action can be taken quickly when I die. Be aware that some illnesses, such as hepatitis or HIV, make donations

---

13   www.humanservices.gov.au

impossible. You will receive by mail an organ donor card that you should keep in an accessible place – your Will file is sensible. There have been cases where young people have been put under duress to donate organs to family members which should not be done.

TRANSPLANT TOURISM

It is possible to obtain transplants in Thailand among other places. It is said that organs are harvested to order. An unfortunate person, likely destitute or homeless, is given a small amount of money (and little after-care) but the cost to the patient can be as much as AUD$250,000. A deterrent is the fact that antibiotic resistance is very widespread in some overseas hospitals. Many such patients need further, often corrective care on their return and some have brought back the antibiotic resistance which has become a great problem in our hospitals. Research well if you need to go down this path. China claims that 90% of their organ transplants are sourced from executed prisoners, but executions seemingly number far less than the transplants taking place. I understand that in China a cornea currently costs $30,000, and a liver $98,000.

Thinking ahead 5: Family matters: personal papers, chattels

Sort. Keep. Digitise. Give. Chuck!

FAMILY DOCUMENTS

Birth, christening, wedding certificates, citizenship papers et al., should always be carefully stored together, not amongst other papers. You should have a large envelope clearly labelled on the front with the list of the certificates it contains. There should be a similar one for any historic birth and marriage certificates – tracing your ancestors is becoming a popular hobby. You can give these papers to a family member to preserve.

Sometimes secrets are revealed at a death, in the Will or in the papers that are left behind. Approach these with care and thought. Some secrets should be allowed to float away on the vast, dark river of lost memories. Others, such as the unrevealed responsibility for a child or mistress, might need to be acknowledged and dealt with. When dealing with an estate, if you come across anything that shocks you think hard before passing it on to a wider audience

FINANCIAL PAPERS, PROFESSIONAL PAPERS

Remember the Tax Office requires you to keep financial records – bank statements, share transaction papers etc. – for seven years. Banks keep easily accessible records for only two years, after that it takes some time (a week, I understand) for records to be accessed from their archives. Some professions, medical for instance, need to keep records for 25 years.

PHOTOGRAPHS AND CORRESPONDENCE

Make sure you have both named and hopefully dated old family photographs. You may be the last person who can tell two old aunts apart or recognise a long-lost uncle. Sort files containing correspondence and personal details. This can be a nightmare, but the only person who knows which things are of real importance is the person who has kept it all. If there is too much, it will all be thrown out unread – items of vital interest along with the rest.

If you hold documents that might be of interest to a public library, but whose significance would escape a casual, hurried sorter, contact them by phone and they will collect. Public libraries, state or university, are patient about sorting and cataloguing a mass of interesting information.

FAMILY HISTORIES, AUTOBIOGRAPHICAL ACCOUNTS

Give a thought to leaving in the Will file some account of your life. The good and the difficult. Now is the time, if you have not done so before, to note down all the information about your family that comes to mind – the things your grandmother told you that cannot be found in records or statistics. The stories about the great-great grandmother who was sad because her three children had emigrated to Australia. They sent letters back but... she never heard their voices again. The stories about those five maiden aunts appearing as such dry twigs on the family tree. A story was passed down in my family about our Indian great-great-grandmother who had rescued our great-great-grandfather, the son of a Scottish Laird, at the ferocious Siege of Lucknow in 1857, and had saved his life by hiding him in a cornfield. He had married her out of gratitude, perhaps, but perhaps also for love. We thought this all sounded a bit, well... corny. But my parents called on the present Laird to find that their family had passed down the story of their visit home. No doubt frozen (we have just one photograph of her – dark haired, corseted), the Indian bride must have been a sensation in the cold, staid Highlands because the visit, unforgotten in their family, was still marvelled at 130 years later! What a story.

A friend reminisced that, when young, he had been in a German boys' choir that was on a tour of England when the Second World War broke out. He had been stranded in England and fostered. He had never seen his family again. He had ended up an internationally acclaimed professor in America. Life must have been a struggle and perhaps for that reason he had never told his own family of this – they did not know anything of his background. What courage. How proud his grandchildren would be if they knew. What a story! Write it, I told him. It's important.

FAMILY RECIPES

I have a small loose-leaf cookbook. Some of the recipes came from my mother, some from friends. To be sure, the recipes tell you how to cook something, but their actual value is in the memories of the feasts, the celebrations, the gatherings they fed... and of the cooks who cooked them. They are an inheritance more precious than gold, and should never be lost.

MEMORABILIA

Itemising your chattels. A tiny grandson rushes to climb the stairs to sit in front of a carved tribal head. He shrieks in terrified glee. I have said to his parents that they might like to choose this on his behalf one day – so that he might remember his visits to me. I have a feeling that they flinch at the prospect! Two children like the same object. I have written which one I feel should have first refusal. Put in family information that might otherwise be lost. That chair was given to your great grandmother on her wedding, the little gold cross that belonged to your grandmother, the blue vase looks valuable, but is a clever fake and so on.

I visited a friend who, like me, has a house full of long-loved, perhaps not valuable, but interesting objects. She laughed. Her children had asked her what would happen when she died. Could she begin to think about the big, big problem that they faced. She had laughed, she said and told them it was their problem to deal with after her death. I have a different attitude. Many of the things I have have little money-value but are of unexpected interest if you know what they are. When I die, I would love to think they could be passed on to other people who would get the same (or even different) pleasure from them as I have done. I am beginning to sort out my books, my things. The same problem: two different answers.

KEEPSAKES

An old friend who was nearly 100, died. A pile of envelopes was found at her death, each with a small gift for everyone she had loved. I do not know how many years they had been prepared and waiting. Neither can I tell you the joy it gave me to know, as I opened mine – a pair of earrings – that she had valued our friendship as much as I had done. It is worth considering if there is anyone in your life who would receive as much pleasure as I did from that gesture.

GRIEVING FOR PARENTS, SIBLINGS

I won't suggest reading the Bible, Shakespeare or Jane Austen for tips, but... nearly. Life has subtle turns and twists. It has ways of leaving you gutted, but it also has glories and joys. A great grief means there has been a great loss. I feel I would rather live with a great loss that not to have had something in my life worth grieving for. An academic suggests a 'flu model' for grief: that grief is unpleasant but relatively short-lived. Normal grieving, he says, on average, should last roughly six months. A bereavement is a life-sentence with time-off for good behaviour if you deal with it well. One of us is wrong. Probably me.

Some people do not stop mourning. Complicated, deep grief which can last for years is a different matter. It is important to get good counselling for such a person.

Thinking ahead 6: Choosing where to live if illness or debility impacts your living choices

It is important at any stage of life to consider future life-options carefully. If possible, consider a change of accommodation before it is actually needed – when decisions often have to be made in a hurry and in a state of stress. If the need to move is sudden – an unforeseen health problem, for instance, it can be very hard to manage satisfactorily.

Quite often the decision to move from a long-term home is triggered by a sudden major change in circumstances: the death of a partner, a financial catastrophe (divorce, perhaps). It may be caused by general debility (can't manage the stairs), a sudden fall, difficulty in shopping or cooking that makes action necessary. There are facilities which provide services ranging from serving meals and overseeing medication through to complete care if bed ridden. The state of health, the family's needs and financial position will all affect the choices a person has available to them. The first instinct when deciding to move may be to choose somewhere where the person has friends or has visited a place that may be familiar. But give thought as to the family members or friends who are most likely to visit – it may be kind to consider moving closer to that person, or nearer to grandchildren so they are not faced with an onerous driving regime. Ask advice from a GP in the area you might consider – they will have the best up-to-date knowledge of suitable facilities. Visit such places before the need arises if possible, as there can be long waiting lists for some.

STAYING PUT

Some people can be very isolated in their own home but moving can also be isolating – the loss of friends, networks, familiar surroundings, a beloved garden, a favourite cafe. The sorrow of sorting and discarding beloved possessions. It may be possible to get help so that a person can stay in their home for longer but be aware this may only delay a necessary decision. Worsening health might make it even harder to move in the future.[14]

COUNCIL/SHIRE SUPPORT

Councils provide and help pay for services that allow the less-well to live safely at home for as long as possible, in order to delay the move to a residential nursing home. Find out what services the person can access in the area – cleaning, gardening, shopping, meals, nurses etc. The local council has many ways of helping. They will come and inspect the home and install (free of charge in many cases) what is needed: handrails or ramps, for example, in the house. A support worker will come to the home three times a week to help a patient shower or dress, perhaps help with cooking, gardening, driving to appointments and shops, house cleaning, meals service and the like. Some low-cost carers provide simple services which can mean they make additional charges for services that other, more expensive providers include as part of their package, so check before you hire.

---

14 'Let's Get Care' is a government program that helps people stay in their homes www.agedcareguide.com.au

RETIREMENT LIVING

Moving to a retirement village – a 'sea change' is popular. Such villages have manageable, independently self-owned houses or units. There are often restaurants/cafe/shopping facilities, communal transport, congenial company and activities. A nurse will be on duty who can organise help in case of emergency. Research has found that many aged-care residents find aged-care living to be a relief from the risks and concerns of living independently. But take care: the contracts can sometimes be 80 pages long. Confusing? They may well be designed to be just that. There can be weekly charges, and extra fees for support services, or for the use of communal areas or amenities. Exit fees can be as high as 40% and any rise in value of the property may go to the company, not the person who owns the unit. Costs can be payable even if the unit is not lived in, until the property is sold. Some places make final deductions, which all make it hard to guess your eventual financial position. Difficulties can occur, for example, if one of a couple needs to raise money for a bond for an aged care facility by using the equity of their home. It can result in the remaining spouse being left without a home or the possibility of providing for their own future care. Most such villages have a resident's committee, it may be sensible to make enquiries from it before you buy. There has been recent government concern about the governance of some chains in particular, it will be interesting to read the report on this when it is published.

AGED CARE FACILITIES, RESIDENTIAL APARTMENTS, TRANSITION LIVING

There are facilities available that cater to differing levels of care. Residential apartments and retirement homes allow you to bring your own furniture and possessions. Some provide kitchens, others provide catering in communal dining rooms, and are like hotels in that you can come and go. You still have independence. The National Ageing Research Institute, run from the Royal Women's Hospital, Melbourne, says that their research shows many aged-care residents find the comfort and safety of communal living is a relief from the risk of living independently.

The owner of a string of Aged Care facilities is clever and kind. Her four criteria are:

1. Nice building
2. Good food
3. Good care
4. *If there's no fun you might as well be dead.*

That last one I love! People often arrive underweight, she says, having found it hard to look after themselves. In good places, dietary preferences are taken into account. They will have dining rooms, perhaps a cafe, and may have visiting hairdressers, manicurists, physiotherapists, weekly Tai Chi and Zumba (exercises performed to music while seated in a chair) for instance and may organise outings and bus tours.

It is good to understand that different Aged Care facilities may cater for different clienteles. She has noticed that in one of the homes which has a high proportion of retired lawyers, judges and the like, the conversation is all about history or literature. Another has a high proportion of tradies. They apparently have a men's shed type of ball. Many have been self employed, working with perhaps only a few employees, and they enjoy the companionship of life in such a facility. Near me, a new Aged Care facility has opened which caters for the LGBTQI+ community. It means that a person does not feel they need to hide who they are.

AGED CARE FACILITIES

Moving to a nursing home may be necessary if a high level of care is needed and death is not imminent: they provide total care and nursing. One source says that a severely disabled man entering a nursing home will on average live for 2.1 years and a woman for 5.8 years.[15]

---

15 www.kincare.com.au and www.tlcagedcare.com.au

FINANCING AGED CARE

Most old age facilities require you to put down a bond. This is a capital sum that will eventually be returned to your estate. There may be a daily charge and charges for extras (a glass of wine at dinner, choice of meal, broader TV coverage etc.,). Check carefully the terms and conditions of places you are considering.

LOW-MEANS RESIDENTS

The financially disadvantaged can obtain government subsidies. This can be complicated, and it is sensible to go to a retirement living and aged care specialist firm such as Aged Care Gurus to ensure you obtain the best advice.

TEMPORARY RESPITE

Many retirement and nursing homes offer temporary stays of a week or so. This is good to give a carer a few days of respite. But it also means the dependent person can try out the facilities and may find they would be happy to make a permanent move while they are still capable of providing input to the downsizing and division of their furniture and possessions.

RESIDENTIAL PARKS, CARAVAN LIVING

Caravan living is becoming popular as a living choice. 'Grey nomads' chase the sun and then return to their permanent home, but some people choose to make the small companionable space of a caravan their home. Often this choice is made because of the low cost, no exit fees, or ongoing costs, but some caravans are being aimed at this market – luxurious, dishwashers... all the comforts of home!

If this appeals, choose a campsite close to transport hubs that give access to major city services (doctors, hospitals etc.,) without having to live near them. People who live in residential parks own their own caravan/demountable homes but rent the land it is on. If only one of a couple remains, there are often very caring communities to support and be of cheer to a single person. There are even clubs formed around this lifestyle. Interestingly, being of no fixed address, I am told such people are not counted in the census. It is not known how many people choose to live this way, but I am told their number is growing. The American film 'Nomadland' (which won the Academy Award for Best Film in 2020, and I have not seen) references this growing trend in the USA and might be of interest if you contemplate this path.

FRIENDSHIP GROUPS

I have heard that some congenial friends group together, buy a hotel, and employ a nurse and a chef between them. It sounds a happy, if complex, solution, but problems can arise if members of the group die, and less congenial people join the group.

CHAPTER FOUR

Dealing with illness and planning end-of-life care

DEALING WITH SERIOUS ILLNESS

Understand that if one of a family is diagnosed with a serious illness, everyone in the family will be affected by it, both emotionally (the loving) and physically (the caring). Do not underestimate the impact of that on you if you are the carer.

Try to make time to accompany a sick person to as many doctor's appointments as you can. My husband had been diagnosed with cancer, but I realised early on that when he visited the doctor on his own, he was hearing only what he wanted to hear, what he could accept and handle. He would come back with, 'The doctor said it was fine' – then hand over more prescriptions. Fine? OK, but why had the doctor felt it was necessary to add all these? We compromised. I would accompany him on alternate appointments. I sat with an unobtrusive pad of paper and wrote down what was said, prescribed, the changes in dose, adverse effects to look out for, foods to be avoided. Often, I would remind him of something the doctor had said, which he had completely forgotten. Sometimes a sick person feels that by going alone to appointments it shows the world they can manage, they are not dependent, that they are not so sick they need to be accompanied like a child.

Make sure the doctor knows how you are feeling. They will know how the patient is but will not know the toll it is taking on you.

It can be hard for an ill person and their family to talk about the situation, but there are very helpful, kind websites to access with good advice that are worth checking out[16].

TALKING TO A PERSON WHO IS TERMINALLY ILL

Two of our oldest friends upon hearing my husband was terminally ill called in for a drink. We talked about the latest political scandal, their children, the weather. They did not refer to the sword hanging over our heads. They left. We caught each other's eyes and said nothing. It would have been kind if they had said sorry. To regret that the treasured friendship was fading, to acknowledge that a major event was in train.

Some people do not want to talk about their approaching end but they and their partner might still be comforted by an acknowledgement that their lives are about to change forever. It is as simple as: "I'm sorry to hear". A friend whose partner is dying of cancer ruefully told me that he has discovered casseroles, hideously congealed, sitting in his letterbox. What he needs more than casseroles is a kind face, a human concern, a knock on the door, the smile that says 'I'm sorry'.

DEALING WITH MEDICATION

When a serious sickness is diagnosed, medication can suddenly be a large part of your life. Be aware that a person who is sick and who may be on multiple medications can appear to be their normal, intelligent selves but may have a very much reduced ability to concentrate, to remember, to function, and their moods may vary dramatically. If there are great changes of mood, tell your doctor.

---

16   www.mariecurie.org.uk

It is important the doctor knows all the medications a patient is taking including over the counter, herbal or Chinese remedies, as some medicines can interact badly. Make sure the doctor knows if a patient drinks alcohol, drives or operates machinery as some medications can make a person drowsy and affect their ability to safely carry on with their normal lives.

If a person takes more than four prescribed medications they should show the scripts to a pharmacist, who will know better than their doctor if any may have an adverse inter-reaction.

A pharmacist told me one of his customers insists on taking all the twenty-seven prescriptions he has been given by his various doctors and specialists – but, he said, that's enough to make anyone ill! That patient has to have regular stays in hospital to detox.

You may be offered the generic version of a drug – identical in every way, they will say. Check with your doctor as some generics are *nearly* but not *quite* the same, there can be slight variations in ingredients. It is cheaper perhaps, *but it also has a different name.* Do not underestimate how hard it can be to keep up to date with all the complicated names that look so different from the ones prescribed. Get the chemist to write down clearly the prescribed name, the generic name, the chemical ingredients and doses, and what it is treating. Then keep this master-list at home. The names and dosages on bottles can be small and hard to read. And even a clever person can get hopelessly confused by trying to remember which is to be taken before or after meals; first thing in the morning, before food, twice a day, three times after meals...

A pharmacist[17] can sometimes help by putting all the pills for a week into a compartmented plastic pill box. It may be necessary to store medication at particular temperatures or securely, so that children cannot access them. Keep a note of side effects or unusual reactions.

It may be useful to know that doctors can arrange a free service

---

17 Supercare Pharmacies have pharmacists available 24/7, and a registered nurse on duty between 6-10pm for free, out-of-hours consultation. www.betterhealth.vic.gov.supercarepharmacies

whereby a pharmacist will call and review medications from around the house – bathroom, bedroom, kitchen; check what the patient is taking, sort to see that medications do not clash and are not out of date. This is especially useful if the patient is likely to be forgetful. If a person travels with medication, remember that some prescriptions need a doctor's letter to be carried – Customs cannot tell if a pill is curative or hallucinogenic – and especially if syringes need to be taken in hand luggage.

Be aware that some people can be addicted to a certain medicine and will go 'doctor shopping' until they find someone willing to prescribe it to them. I know a nurse who is very concerned that her mother doctor-shops for Fentanyl, a highly addictive opioid that makes her noticeably unsteady on her feet and liable to fall. It is extremely toxic and has been implicated in many deaths.

DISPOSING OF MEDICINES

Always take excess or unused medicines, even unneeded household chemicals to a pharmacy for disposal. Some have to be disposed of with special care. Many medicines are in sealed packets, which can be re-used or given to a charitable organisation. You may even receive a refund. Flushing them down a toilet is a no-no: it means they will enter the water supply where they can do harm. Injectable morphine, especially, has to be removed from the house after a death in case it is misused by anyone.

PAIN MANAGEMENT

If a patient is living with pain and the medication prescribed is not of sufficient benefit, a pain management specialist may suggest it is preferable to be monitored in hospital by professional carers.

MONEY

I have said before: remember, it may be sensible to make provisions if there is a possibility the person who usually pays medical fees etc., is likely to become incapable of doing so.

BEING A CARER FOR SOMEONE AT HOME – RESPITE

It can happen that well-meaning (or otherwise) family members can discuss and battle between themselves and not include the person concerned in discussing preferred outcomes as to future care or residential choices. People in hospital often beg to come home. Be objective. Inform yourself of their current condition. Their nurse (more than their doctor) may be able to judge if you will be able to manage. How's your back? Will you be able to lift them if they fall? Can they walk as far as the bathroom? Could you help them there? Change incontinence nappies? Do you have stairs? Are you aware of their latest medications (often changed in hospital) their names and doses? Can you cope with their pain and relieve it? Will you need/are you able to employ help? How much (both hours and cost)?

Most hospitals have a system called HITH (Hospital in the Home) whereby you can be registered with them as a patient but can obtain ongoing nursing care, physiotherapy, and the like, in your own home. If a sick person is able to return home, the hospital will send someone to check that the home is suitable:

- that couches and beds are at the right height
- there is a seat in the shower
- suggest where rails might be necessary
- remove rugs that can be tripped over
- ensure there is a secure place to store morphine etc., if needed.

You may need to hire special hospital beds or commodes, walkers, wheelchairs... Explore the internet for what you need. Equipment can be delivered to you, often at short notice, and set up and removed when no longer needed. Where possible, choose a room near a bathroom with a view out of a window. Put in comfortable chairs so visitors are made welcome.

It has recently become possible to install software packages that monitor activities such as getting up, eating, showering, so that a relative, say, can monitor an aged person from a distance.

If the patient is a smoker, be aware that nursing staff have the legal right to refuse to enter the home concerned.

AGED CARE ASSESSMENT SERVICES, (ACAS, VICTORIA) (ACAT, OTHER STATES)

It is important to be aware of this useful government service. If someone is aged it is good to register with this service *long before* you imagine you (or your parents) need to make use of what is on offer. It can take up to a year for an assessment to go through. Once you have been accepted, you can make use of this service whenever you need it, therefore it is sensible to register when you are still well, and long before you think it is necessary. Your (their) GP will come to the home to make an assessment of your (their) condition and keep a strictly confidential record of it. The paperwork does not lapse, and once registered with this service, many benefits become available.

For instance, if a person becomes unable to cope due to arthritis/osteoporosis, or if the patient or their main carer has a sudden accident – they fall and break a hip/wrist for example – and cannot cope, if they have been registered with ACAS the carer or both can access free government-paid respite or transition care for 60 days while the problem, hopefully, is cured.

This gives a period in which to assess the situation and decide what may need to happen next. The aim is to return the person to their home, but if that is not possible it gives time to come to a decision about the best way forward. ACAS will also provide subsidised care in the community: shopping, cleaning services, visits to the bank etc. The service is approachable and friendly, and intended to help a person live at home safely for longer.

There is a means test, and the person is allocated to one of four stages of assistance. An ACAS assessment does not cost anything and does not commit you to anything, but you cannot be admitted to a nursing home until you have had this assessment.[18]

---

18   www.myagedcare.gov.au or 1800 200 422

Take care to record your receipt number, as this service is very careful about confidentiality.

I am fit and well. But I have applied for registration under this scheme. It is not needed, but my children find it comforting to know that I am thinking ahead.

BE CLEAR

A person *also* needs to be assessed and enrolled in their local shire/council system, which provides care such as a visiting nurse to help with personal hygiene, shopping, cleaning, day respite, excursions and the like. A local councillor/shire representative will visit to assess the specific requirements.

USEFUL SITES

www.myagedcare.vic.gov.au
is a most useful one stop shop. Tel **1800 200 422**

www.publicadvocate.vic.gov.au
discusses powers of guardianship

www.acptalk.com.au
Advanced Care Planning provides sensitive religious and cultural advance care planning for many religious denominations including secular

AMBULANCE SUBSCRIPTION

Pensioners, with concession cards/pension number are well covered, but many people have discovered there is much small print and some have found themselves paying large bills – $400 for ambulance transport home, 4kms from the hospital or $8,000 for helicopter transport from a ski resort to a major town hospital. My local service – Ambulance Victoria – is only partially government funded, and such subscriptions help keep these vital services afloat.[19]

---

19 ambulance.vic.gov.au

PALLIATIVE CARE

Many palliative care nurses feel that their profession is not understood by the public at large. Palliative care nurses and doctors aim to improve the quality of life for someone living with a terminal condition. Their focus is on helping a patient live as well as they can with their illness, minimising suffering rather than finding a cure. They are not frightened by death. You can ask for palliative care at any time after you have a diagnosis. Palliative care can increase, reduce, or stop as your needs change, and is not limited to the last days or weeks of life. A palliative care nurse can advise on financial, family or spiritual matters that may concern the patient. They can soothe patient worries such as wondering if they are a burden on their family; will their children be all right; how long do they have; how to tell people. I have heard that some will even take notes and write your autobiography.

Palliative care nurses know who can help. If you can, talk to one. I found they follow a calling rather than a job. They seem to be the most intuitive and caring and kind people. They are used to dealing with all the unasked questions and turmoil of this stage of a person's life, whereas the patient and their family may never have had experience of this type of situation. They provide a supportive communication network that you can ring at any time of day or night. They will come in to bathe or dress the patient, renew dressings if necessary. They can provide aged-care assessment and advise if you need further assistance. The patient will need a referral from a doctor or hospital to access this service. Most palliative care services are free but it is always good to ask about costs.[20]

There may be a short term problem with wound dressings after a fall or surgical procedure. Not everyone is fortunate to have private healthcare insurance, but if you do it is worth checking to see if your health fund can provide this service, especially if it allows a patient to go home quicker from hospital. This also applies to physiotherapy in the home following a joint replacement.

If a friend looks frailer than usual it could be kind to ask if you could

---

20 www.pallcarevic.asn.au or 03 9662 9644 (during business hours)

drive them to a doctor's appointment or offer to do their shopping. This is a non-intrusive acknowledgement of the value their friendship has played in your life and lets them know they are loved.

If a sick person is to be left alone for some time it may be sensible to acquire a device such as a security *mCare Watch*, which allows the wearer to call any of three people with just one press.

Live Life is another recommended emergency personal alarm. It has a one-off cost and comes with a GPS, which means that it works if you are out and about. It has a sim card so your documented contacts can phone you via the pendant alarm.

IF YOU ARE A CARER

A carer is someone who provides unpaid care to a person who cannot manage without their assistance, whether they are young, old, sick, or disabled. If you are caring for someone who needs constant attention, it will not help matters if, by neglecting yourself, you become ill too. It is hard to feel strong and healthy when your life's love is sitting, failing in a chair. It is inevitable that you will lose fitness yourself over a long vigil. You might find it impossible to go off for the walk that would do you more good than anything else. Try to have a coffee with a friend out of earshot of the patient, out of the house, have a breather. You have to shop. When you do, take an extra ten minutes to power walk around. Your patient will not notice the time, but you will notice the difference.

> Remember: That the survivor has to survive!

RESPITE, CARERS ALLOWANCE

If you are providing unpaid care to a child, partner, relative or friend who cannot manage without your assistance due to profound disabilities, you may be eligible for a government carers allowance. You can claim a carers allowance online via the Centrelink website. The allowance is not means tested, does not affect your super, your pension, or your taxable income. Currently it is $A124.70 per fortnight.

Many councils provide temporary respite care, to give the carer a rest. These sites provide a variety of respite, care, either at home or in a residential facility for a broad range of needs, ages and disabilities. A great deal of help is available.[21]

If you or the patient begin to suffer from depression, there are services available to you.[22]

DEMENTIA

Dementia is on the verge of overtaking heart problems as the leading cause of death in Australia. Statistics vary, but 10% of people over 65 and 30% over 80 are said to suffer from this debilitating disease. The average life span after a diagnosis is said to be seven years. New treatments are being developed which seem to slow the symptoms, but these are not always the get-out-of-jail card that they appear.

I know two people who have been given advanced Alzheimer's treatment. One who, after the most advanced American treatment, now recognises me. Her husband is thrilled with the marginal improvement in her condition, but her children are not. She is alive, certainly, but she is helpless, reduced. She is not the same mother they loved. The other, a dear friend, had a daughter who was a physician, who obtained advanced medication to slow the course of her mother's Alzheimer's, but she is aware she has it. She, who had a vivid, incisive intelligence and was always the life and soul of any party, has sat at home for six years now. She does not like to see people, she is embarrassed, empty.

Social isolation is one of the most difficult consequences of this affliction. I know that my friend has considered suicide. She is living a half-life, which she hates. The intention of the family – the chance of regaining normality – had been kindly meant, but no treatment and a faster route to oblivion might, I feel have been actually preferable for her. (And remember, I love her).

The time before diagnosis can be most difficult, with personality

---

[21] www.carergateway.gov.au and www.humanservices.gov.au
[22] www.beyondblue.org.au and Lifeline

changes such as aggression becoming evident. The diagnosis can come as an almost comforting confirmation that the differences have a reason. A person whose partner develops dementia or Alzheimer's often feels they are shut out of their friendship circle, they can feel socially marooned. A friend whose husband has dementia says she feels people are reluctant to enquire about him. If he was suffering from cancer, she feels, they might show more concern.

One partner may find it is hard to do things on their own, especially as their significant other is still living. Living with a person who suffers from dementia is especially hard because there has not been a death but the partner grieves as deeply as if there had been. Dementia can give rise in the carer to sadness, resentment at the time, the care needed and guilt at the resentment. It is difficult for all.

Families with a member diagnosed with dementia often worry that they may one day be diagnosed with the disease. Age, I am told, raises the chances of Alzheimer's more than family history. You can be tested, but I understand that the testing will only tell you if you have the Alzheimer's gene, it will not tell you if you are at risk of developing it.

There is excellent support available.[23]

I have not gone into this subject in depth because both the needs of the patient and the services offered in their area can vary greatly.

ASSISTED DEATH

Legislation to allow the compassionate possibility of assisted suicide, euthanasia or assisted dying is currently much debated around the world, but I am told it is a more complex problem that it appears to be on the surface. One concern is that such legislation could lead to 'elder abuse': pressure from relatives and concern that if an older person feels they are a burden they may feel that they have a duty to die. (One doctor is quoted as saying that people can easily be coerced when they are vulnerable; he uses the phrase "Please put mum out of my misery".)

---

23 National Dementia Helpline 1800 100 500 and www.dementia.org.au

Differentiate between:

- *assisted suicide:* where an individual may be seriously disabled but have many years to live
- *euthanasia:* where a doctor administers lethal medication at the request of someone who may or may not be terminally ill
- *assisted dying:* in which a physician acts on the settled wish of a patient who continues to suffer despite the best palliative care by providing him or her with medication for self-administration at a time of their own choosing.

Where Assisted Dying legislation exists – including The Netherlands, Switzerland, Quebec (Canada), Oregon (United States) – there are stringent controls and surprisingly few people are assisted in this way, but it concerns some that both The Netherlands and Oregon have gradually extended the law to include ever-widening groups. Very ill patients, I am told, often find it comforting to know that assisted suicide is accessible but apparently few avail themselves of it. My newspaper reports that in the State of Victoria 500 people have used the Victorian assisted dying laws since they were introduced. Of these 58% who died through this scheme self-administered their medication, 10% had it administered by their medical practitioner and 32% died without needing to take it. Dr Rodney Syme, a well-known euthanasia advocate has said that many people may not need to take the lethal dose but that the mere fact of having it gives them a sense of control over their condition.

Interestingly, COVID-19 fuelled an anxiety around dying and saw a surge (applications more than doubled) in terminally ill people asking to end their lives at home, amid fears the virus could thwart their hopes for a swift, painless death surrounded by loved ones, instead of in a hospital isolated from their family. Protection for the doctor treating a patient under such circumstances is often needed: if 'double effect' medicine is prescribed, if continuous palliative sedation is given, or if a doctor withholds or withdraws futile treatments, there can be room to challenge the treatment suggested.

CHOOSING A FUNERAL COMPANY

It is sensible at any stage of life to choose a preferred funeral company and have the information accessible in case of sudden need. In the next section I will explain why it is important and how to go about choosing one.

CHAPTER FIVE

Dealing with the actual death

'Oh, to be old again,' said the young corpse

~Stanislaw Jerzy Lee

Part 1: Information about some of the choices that are available in disposing of the dead

DYING IN A HOSPITAL OR NURSING HOME

Many hospitals and aged-care facilities either have no mortuaries or have closed them to save money. Hospitals try to allocate a single room for a dying patient, and they try to allow a grieving family time with the body. They will have a chaplaincy or social services department that can be greatly comforting, if needed. Hospitals often have people waiting on trolleys for a bed and there can be pressure to remove a deceased person. Some hospitals will ask on the admittance of a patient if there is a preferred funeral company, especially if the patient is old or very sick. But if not, they may call one of their choice that is likely to be a large chain which will have a driver available at any time of day or night. Once that happens it is hard to get the body back in order to employ a funeral director of your choice. So it is sensible to have a preferred company chosen and the name handy (in the Will file perhaps, and also with the person who holds the Power of Medical Attorney).

DYING AT HOME

If a death takes place at home, contact your doctor or the police. If the deceased has seen a doctor in the last three to six months, the doctor will usually issue a locum or doctor's certificate. The body cannot be removed by a funeral director until this has been issued.

NECESSARY PAPERWORK

The hospital will obtain the certificate if death takes place there. The funeral director will send the doctor's certificate to the Registry of Births, Deaths and Marriages who will issue the official death certificate some weeks later. You will need several copies of this that need to be properly witnessed and endorsed to settle the deceased's affairs.

If it is deemed that there are suspicious circumstances surrounding the death, the paperwork is sent to the coroner who will need to make a decision as to the cause of death and whether there is a need for further investigation. The coroner will then issue a certificate to allow the funeral to proceed.

AUTOPSIES

If the cause of death is not straightforward a coroner may decide that an autopsy (sometimes called a post-mortem examination) be conducted after considering information provided by police pathologists or other forensic specialists. Bodies admitted to most mortuaries are scanned upon admission and the findings of such a scan may eliminate the need for an autopsy. The coroner will direct that an autopsy be performed only if it will assist in the investigation into the person's death and/or the circumstances surrounding their death. The senior next-of-kin has the right to object to an autopsy being performed (on religious grounds for instance) and if the coroner believes it should still be performed, the senior next-of-kin can apply to the Supreme Court for an order preventing it.

Certain religious traditions include swift burial (Jewish and Muslim, for instance), and forbid autopsies. The autopsy in such a case may be limited to a blood test (to check for poison). If the coroner cannot establish the cause of death, they have the discretion to ask for an autopsy. This can be challenged in the Supreme Court, and a decision is usually handed down within 24 hours.

Such applications are dealt with on their merits and may be successful. If the coroner directs an autopsy be performed and there is no objection, or if the objection is unsuccessful, a pathologist (a medical specialist trained in the science of looking at the effects of the body of disease or trauma) will carry out an external and internal examination of the body. The major organs of the body are examined and specimens may be taken for more detailed examination. This may include tests for infection (microbiology), changes in body tissue or organs (histology), medications, drugs or poisons (toxicology). These tests are carried out on samples of blood and tissue that are taken and retained for that purpose.

The person's body is treated with respect at all times. From the date of admission and following the autopsy the body will be released back to the family in five to seven days. The autopsy findings are generally available after six weeks. Accordingly, if a coroner is involved it may be several months before a cause of death can be registered and a death certificate issued by Births, Deaths and Marriages (BDM). In these circumstances the coroner or BDM can provide an interim death certificate confirming that a death has occurred. This may assist the family in administering financial affairs.

I asked a coroner what the strangest case was he had ever had. He laughed. He had, he said, come in to work to find a huge shark on the slab... together with a human arm which had been found in its mouth. The rest of the body was never found, and the body remains unidentified.

CORONER'S REPORTS

These can take six months to arrive in the post. Printed on the outside will be a warning that you should not open then or read them when you are alone as they can be distressing. They can be complex. If you receive a coroner's report, ask a family member or friend to go with you to your GP to get help in understanding it.

CHOOSING A FUNERAL COMPANY

Death can happen unexpectedly. It is sensible to decide on a funeral company long before a death is expected. The funeral industry self-regulates and it is worth doing some research. Wherever the death occurs, choose a funeral company that is a member of one of the regulating organisations. In Australia, the Australian Funeral Directors Association (AFDA), in the United Kingdom the National Society of Allied Independent Funeral Directors (SAIF), in the United States the National Funeral Directors Association (NFDA). Your local funeral home may be good, but a preferred funeral director is usually happy to travel a fair distance to help. It could be sensible (take a friend for support) to interview funeral companies near you before you have need of one. For interest, if nothing else.

I went to talk to Mr Nigel Davies, chairman of the Justice Department Round Table to the Funeral Industries, and director of Lonergan & Raven Funeral Directors. I was both amazed and fascinated about some of the things he told me.

Broadly there are three kinds of funeral firms.

CORPORATE CHAINS

These companies attempt to maintain a high standard. They provide 24-hour support. They have 24-hour rosters, and this means that sometimes you face a different member of staff on each consultation, even though they have systems that provide a continuity of advice. Large chains have been accused of lumping all costs together so that it is impossible to compare costs between funeral companies. They will not give quotes over the phone, expecting that families will not be in a position to spend time making comparisons.

SMALLER FAMILY-BASED COMPANIES

These companies allocate one member of staff to each family so that there is more personal support and a sympathetic continuity of service. They may have less fancy facilities, smaller chapels and such, and their charges are usually less than those of larger firms.

'BRIEFCASE OPERATORS'

Mobile phone, station wagon, and refrigerator, who come and go and rarely have the proper facilities or staff. Avoid these.

DO-IT-YOURSELF, NATURAL BURIALS

You do not legally have to employ a funeral director. Indeed, home funerals though small in number are growing in popularity. It is common sense to keep the heating off and the air conditioning on if it is hot, perhaps bags of ice under the blanket. If you prefer to be independent, you have to pay the doctor (for the certificate), crematorium, cemetery, upfront. I am told you also need to obtain public liability cover. If the deceased has suffered from HIV or a communicable disease such as Diphtheria, you need to know that special, labelled body-bags have to be used.

Many people who lose a young child like the body to be kept at home for as long as possible. The funeral service can take place at home with the deceased then taken directly to the cemetery or crematorium. It is necessary to make a booking with both. You can drive the body yourself, but most cemeteries will only accept a body which arrives in a coffin and in a hearse, so take the time to check.[24]

DIRECT DEPOSITION

There is a trend to less expensive funerals. Direct deposition is becoming more popular. Many people (2% in the United Kingdom, 7-10% in Australia, and reportedly mostly from higher socio-economic

---

24   www.gatheredhere.com.au/green-funerals-australia

backgrounds) choose this option. The body of the deceased is taken directly to the crematorium and cremated. You need not attend. If you do, you can sing, clap or cry, but there is no service. You can then organise whatever commemorations you choose. This is the cheapest option for disposing of a body.[25] David Bowie, that great singer, chose to do this.

EMBALMING

There are various forms of embalming, i.e. partial and full. The procedure resembles a blood transfusion or dialysis. Full embalming (expensive) is not usually needed, unless the body is to be buried in an above-ground vault or mausoleum, in which case full arterial embalming is necessary by law. If the body is to be kept for a longer time than usual – if members of the family need to come from abroad, for instance – then, if viewing the body is part of their custom, it is advisable to embalm. Usually only partial embalming is needed. Along with slowing the process of decomposition, it restores a natural appearance which may be desirable if the body is to be viewed after a severe illness for instance.

VIEWING THE BODY

Some traditions have a requirement that the family and friends view the body. If the body is to be viewed, you might want to provide clothing. Certain cultural groups (Irish, Macedonian) traditionally sit around the body for several days. After that time the funeral director can be asked to collect the deceased and keep the body at the funeral company's precinct until the funeral occurs.

REPATRIATION (SENDING A BODY OR ASHES TO ANOTHER COUNTRY FOR BURIAL):

Different countries have different documentation needs and requirements. If the deceased is to be repatriated, the Health Department requires the body to be fully embalmed before it is put on an airplane. The deceased's passport (necessary for purposes of

---

25 www.bereavementassistance.org.au

identification) should be sent back with the body. Airlines charge by weight. A specially lined coffin is needed, with the body sealed in an impermeable covering, and the coffin must be put in a crate. This is all very heavy and therefore very expensive to freight. A cheaper alternative is to cremate the body, and fly with the ashes, or send them by mail. Make enquiries. You will not be allowed to fly with ashes in a sealed urn as Customs could suspect that this was a method of concealing a gun or drugs. You need to comply with the laws of the country from which the body/ashes are sent and also the one in which they will arrive. This can take a great deal of time to sort out.

It may be useful to know that FA Albin & Sons (funeral directors in the United Kingdom) have a multilingual staff with approved agents in over 100 countries who can arrange repatriation or exhumation worldwide, they will deal with permits and documentation.[26]

DISCUSSING FUNERAL DETAILS

Funeral directors are most accepting of individual requirements, and cemeteries cater for all religions. I asked Mr Davies about the variety of traditional expectations he had had to accommodate in his career, he said: 'when I stopped counting – there were more than 200.'

The strangest, in a Western context, was the couple who asked for an 'air burial' – a Bombay-style platform where the body is exposed to scavenging birds. The bones, then clean, in their tradition could be respectfully disposed of. Told that this was not acceptable under local law, as bodies had to be buried in the earth, they replied, 'How *disgusting*'.

Funeral directors insist on having more than one person present when funeral plans are discussed. One person will be designated the *responsible person*. He or she has the final say in arrangements and is also responsible for making the payments. There is a lot to decide and it is helpful to have a relative or friends who can remember, remind, discuss and corroborate the details when everyone is in a state of upset.

---

26 www.albins.co.uk

Make sure that your budgetary limitations are understood. Many funeral homes have opaque pricing structures and may quote an inclusive price for the services provided. Obtain an itemised list of the services you have agreed upon so that in the distress of the moment you know exactly what you are paying for. Be aware of 'up-selling' – the encouragement to choose more expensive options. Some funeral companies provide cars as a matter of course. Others say their staff have to arrive at the venue in their personal cars and may be happy to collect old or frail mourners on the way there. If cars are not provided, take taxis. It is not clever to drive yourself in a state of agitation.

PAYMENT

Funerals can differ widely in cost. The average cost in Australia is $6,000. Fees comprise the funeral director's fees, cemetery or cremation costs, coffin, caterer, to name but a few. Interestingly, prices quoted online are about a quarter less than those quoted face-to-face.

Payment for all third-party costs – priest or celebrant's fees, press notices etc., are required to be paid at the time of the event. Some funeral companies will allow payment in instalments in certain cases of hardship, but check with them. If the deceased has an accident or life insurance policy, some of these expenses may be covered by it. The deceased's bank will cover the costs of a funeral from their funds if a receipt from the Funeral Home is shown to them.[27]

PAUPER'S BURIAL, DESTITUTE BURIAL

The destitute may be cremated, or buried in an unmarked grave with, perhaps, two others in simple chipboard coffins. In many cases their identity may be unknown. The Brotherhood of St Laurence assures me that a prayer is said over each coffin, individually. That is comforting to know.

PRE-PAID, PRE-ARRANGED FUNERALS

Some people like to pre-purchase a grave site or get pleasure putting

---

27 www.gatheredhere.com.au will help you to compare prices in your area.

money into a dedicated account to cover costs of their funeral. If you like planning, the funeral company of your choice will give you forms to complete long before your death, listing your preferences for such things as venue, music, flowers, and anything else you'd like. One father left instructions that there were to be two huge bunches of coloured balloons for his two young children to release as his coffin was driven off. (This is now illegal, as the balloons popping often far away and often out to sea, have been proven to be a hazard to wildlife). Fill in the forms, put them in your 'Will' file. If you pre-pay, the money is tightly regulated: money you pay in is invested in friendly societies. Read the fine print with care.

FUNERAL INSURANCE

This is not recommended. Mr Davies explained you pay a premium which, over the years, can amount to more than six times the total cost of a conventional funeral. Worst of all, if you read the small print, some policies cease when the insurer is 90 years old. The contributions paid are then forfeited. Take care.

CHOICES: RELIGIOUS/SECULAR

There are many options for funerals – religious, church, synagogue, mosque, for instance. Or secular: the funeral chapel, humanist, for those wishing non-religious alternatives.

Religious or cultural beliefs dictate many of the choices and preferences open to a bereaved family. Many of us have wide friendship bases and it is good to be aware of traditions different from our own, so in Section 8 I describe some of the many customs you may need to be aware of. It may matter very much to the older members of a family to see that customs are upheld. Religious services usually follow a tried and true, familiar formula on such occasions. Civil celebrants are free to be more flexible and to accept input from the bereaved's family. I have been to very good, creative and interesting services held by celebrants, but also one which was not so good. I suppose that could have been due to input from the family concerned.

CIVIL CELEBRANTS

Australia was the first country to recognise that some people found the obligatory use of a priest was hypocritical. In 1973 Lionel Murphy, when he was Attorney General under the Whitlam government, brought in legislation so that Civil celebrants had the right to celebrate marriages and deaths in secular services.

Priests had been male authority figures, and it was recognised that female celebrants might be welcome in many cases. Janice Tully was one of the first appointed in 1979. She has dealt with literally thousands of weddings and deaths. Janice has a steady, calm, common sense about her which must be a comfort when facing an upsetting ordeal like a funeral; she has a jolly cheer that is wonderful at a wedding. She holds a BA in Theology and majored in pastoral counselling. A hard part of her job, she says, is to stop tears welling up in cases of great poignancy – burying a small child lost to illness, for instance. Celebrants are trained to conceal emotions but talk to one and they all have memories that are raw and unforgettable.

What shines through is how much she cares and how much pleasure it gives her to be of support in both practical matters and counselling when needed.

Be aware that anyone can call themselves a celebrant. The industry is not regulated, so ask the funeral company for one they recommend.

WEBCASTING

An increasing number of funerals in the United Kingdom are being webcast, or put on Zoom but there can be a downside to this. Paul Allcock, president of the Society of Allied and Independent Funeral Directors (UK), has said that it is "wonderful for those relatives who live abroad, but there is also the danger of pandering to people's laziness and enabling them not to attend personally and sharing their condolences, which is such an important part of the grieving process".

COFFINS AND CASKETS

A coffin is tapered with a flat top, while a casket is rectangular with a hinged, domed lid. If you intend to place items such as medals on top, choose a flat-topped coffin. Our undertaker arrived with a brochure (some funeral directors have their catalogues available on the internet) showing their range of caskets from Eco coffins (made out of cardboard, willow, wool), veneered particle board to solid wood with a wide range of prices (up to $50,000 for the gilded, red-satin padded one as ordered, he said, for a local, famous, recently exit-ed criminal).

Cardboard coffins from China sound a good choice but with the air miles involved are not as environmentally friendly as they appear and should be avoided. Light coloured coffins have become popular, with Texta pens handed out so mourners can cover the coffin with signatures or loving messages before it is driven away. White compressed wool coffins are also superb to graffiti. Wicker coffins are becoming *chic*, but I have heard they can creak alarmingly if the body is heavy. Remember that metals (handles, plaques) have to be removed before a coffin is cremated. Attitudes to coffins vary greatly: many of Asian descent believe the coffin will be the eternal home of their loved one. They wish to make it as beautiful as they can to honour that person. The Scots tend to be austere. Mediterranean taste may tend to the ornate. A Jewish coffin is simple, plain wood – you leave the world in the same way you entered it – with nothing.

Sometimes it is appropriate to commission a special casket such as when a young boy died of cancer and his parents chose a jolly coffin lacquered in the colours of his favourite footy team. I think it made it easier for his young friends, my son amongst them, that he was sent off with such notice taken of his life and loves. A complete contrast recently was the funeral of a superb designer. Killed in a car crash, he was the maker of the famous aluminium Fink jug. His artist friends made him a wonderful coffin – recycled planking with multi-coloured anodised aluminium from his workshop. It was beautiful, putting his life in context, bringing tears of love and care. A highly artistic friend in the pink of health told me she had commissioned her own coffin from a well-known graffiti artist. I was just about to say "I can't wait to see it", when I remembered that when I did, she'd be in it. Some things are best left unsaid.

MAKE YOUR OWN COFFIN

You can make your own coffin[28], but some places have strict regulations that must be adhered to. Coffins have to be waterproof and made of certain materials. Contact your local Occupational Health and Safety (OH&S) for details.

Kiwi Coffin Club, Rotorua, New Zealand: Janet Keen found she went to the funerals of vibrant, vital people and their funerals were... dull. She advertised for people to help make individual coffins, and was inundated with handy people who were able, clever with their hands and with kindness and humour in their hearts. New Zealand now has many Coffin Clubs (*Dying* for new members... putting the *Fun* into *fun*erals...). Members are retirees (typically) who get together to make three coffins in a day, which sell for $350 each. Plain timber, they are meant to be decorated: Elvis, WWII Spitfires, camouflage, flowers, footy club, photos. You can use them, they say, as coffee tables or put shelves in for books until they are needed. The nicest part of the website says: *coffee – lunch – laughs – cuddles*. If it was near me I'd join in a shot! A make-your-own coffin club has recently opened in Tasmania.

SHROUDS

In many places, burial within 24 hours is customary. In Muslim, Indian, Buddhist and many Eastern religions, bodies are wrapped in shrouds before they are cremated or buried. Many Jews are buried in Tachrichim – shrouds. Because of decomposition shrouds are really only suitable for use where a quick burial or cremation is customary.

When my daughter died, the Funeral Home was so kind. Would I like to choose a dress for her to be buried in? We debated. We sorted. We chose. I stood holding it in my hands. And then I put it down. How

---

[28] www.northwoodscasket.com provides build-your-own instructions for a coffin.

could anyone else dress that body I had so loved? Manhandle her cold arms into the sleeves? I rang them. I want her wrapped *gently* in a shroud I said. They told me that this had been the most usual form of burial until the 1980s, when a preference had crept in for a body to be clothed. Perhaps this is due to the open coffins often shown in Hollywood gangster films. Strange how customs slowly alter.

PLACES FOR FUNERALS

Both Janice Tully and Nigel Davies have conducted funerals in usual places: on beaches, on hills. It is often possible to get permission for the actual funeral service to be held at a sports arena or the owner's enclosure at a racecourse, for example, with the coffin then removed for burial or to a crematorium.

BURIAL OR CREMATION

About 65% of families nowadays ask for cremation if it is available. In country areas, distant from crematoriums, burials are more common. Cremation was introduced to Australia in Adelaide 1903, and in Sydney in 1923.

CREMATION

Although the deceased is delivered to a chapel in the Crematorium and disappears before the eyes of the mourners often through a curtained aperture which closes behind the coffin, the deceased is not cremated there but is taken by special transport to the incinerator where the cremation is performed. Several coffins may be cremated at the same time, but each is labelled and in a dedicated part of the chamber, so that the individual ashes are kept separate. Interestingly, I am told that having your own funeral pyre is not illegal, provided it is a one-off, and that it is not on land that keeps having them. (My comment: "!") But please check before doing so.

It is interesting to note that pacemakers have to be removed before cremation, as they explode when heated. This is organised by the funeral director. Leicester Crematorium (United Kingdom) has raised thousands of pounds for charity by saving the bits of metal

– coffin handles, steel hips, replacement knee joints, for instance – frequently found among ashes to be recycled into such things as road signs, motorway barriers and lampposts.

After incineration is completed, the remains are put into a machine with big steel balls which grinds remaining bones into ashes that have the texture of crystalline salt. Ashes usually weigh between two and four kilograms depending on the physique of the deceased. They will be returned to the family in a sealed urn. Do you get back the actual ashes of your loved one? Crematoriums promise that each body is cremated in a named area and that the ashes you receive are those of your loved one. I have a friend whose mother had lived her whole life with shrapnel in her spine after being caught in a London blitz. Being curious and having a military disposition, he sieved the ashes he was given and found no shrapnel. Perhaps the ashes had been sieved before being given to him? But were they hers?

Does it matter? *Ashes to ashes, dust to dust.* Those ashes conceived you. Either with love and calculation or in a wild moment of passion. They gave you birth, suckled you and were kind or horrid as the case may be. It is remarkable, apparently, how many men facing traumatic battlefront deaths are reported as crying out to their mothers as they lie dying – their primal, initial, and sometimes only source of love and comfort. Does it matter if these ashes are your particular person? If you are logical, it does not. But we have hearts, and I think it is possible to argue that it does.

BURIAL

Burial costs about four times more than a cremation. You can buy a grave site in advance, even a family plot. Your right to that grave site lasts forever. A grave site will usually take two coffins, but you can ask for it to be deeper so it can eventually accommodate three coffins. You need to ask before the first burial. It is possible to put up to six sets of ashes into such a grave in the future. Many people forget that a relative has bought a burial plot: check if any family members have done so and make sure a record of it is kept – in their Will file perhaps – so it is easily accessible when needed. Many cemeteries employ staff to trace unused plots, which they are glad to buy back.

Recently, a much-loved young man was buried. The family had to stand around while a gravedigger was called to dig the hole bigger. He had been six foot four inches tall. The funeral home had accommodated his height in a longer coffin but had neglected to inform the gravedigger. Things like this should not happen, but they do.

WAR VETERANS

The RSL (Returned and Services League) will provide a graveside service with the national flag and a brass plaque. Also, they will help with funeral costs in cases where this is a problem.

BURIAL ON PRIVATE LAND

If you wish to bury a loved one on the beloved property they spent a lifetime building, you should know that the farm has to be at least 80 hectares in size. Permission (which can take ten months) has to be given by the Department of Human Services, and the grave site has to be put on the property title as a cemetery. You should be aware that this can complicate the future sale of the property.

Once, when I visited a beautiful and famous country property, I admired a magnificent bank of roses. I was laughingly told "Grandfather is buried up there". Fine. But that property has now been sold. Was grandfather dug up respectfully and taken with the family? Was he left *in situ*, one day perhaps to surprise the new owner? Can you imagine the amazement, the shock: *Bones*...was this an ancient tribal burial or perhaps... a murder? Police or archaeologist?

THE REQUIREMENTS OF DIFFERENT RELIGIONS.

All cultural groups and religions have different traditions to mark the rites of passage – initiations, christenings, Bar-Mitzvahs, marriages, death... I list some of these in Section 8. It is good to be aware of different customs and sensitivities.

LGBTQI+ COMMUNITY

It may be that a person has followed a lifestyle that their family or religious tradition might not approve of or wish to acknowledge. Many women and men have been excluded by families from attending the funeral of their life partner. A 'partner' will sometimes not be recognised as next-of-kin unless there is legal documentation acknowledging that the partnership exists or if they hold Powers of Attorney.

SUICIDES

Suicide leaves a terrible legacy for those who remain. Guilt – could it have been prevented? Rage – at the loss, the waste, the selfishness, the betrayal, perhaps of years of love and care. The agony of 'What if...'. Shame means that sometimes a mourner will not admit that a death was suicide. This can lead to years of social isolation. It may be necessary to try to accept that the person who is gone may have had good reason to feel they could not endure longer life.

Certain religions and clerics will not bury suicides. If a priest is desired, the funeral home may be able to suggest one who is flexible on this matter, but many priests prefer not to be told. One priest I know, Dr Ames, is willing to hold a service for someone who has committed suicide. He says he always ends by saying a prayer commending their soul to 'merciful' God. He was tackled on this: he says that while in his opinion taking one's own life is not good, and many in society condemn it, no-one can know the grief and unresolved problems that drive someone to take such action. He says God is merciful and will extend mercy when it is deserved. That deeply kind, compassionate approach would no doubt be of huge consolation to the family and other mourners who inevitably face such an occasion with greatly conflicting emotions. Good man.

TRAUMA, DRUG OVERDOSE, CAR CRASH, MURDER

Death under such circumstances may be accompanied by law enforcement officers, the legal system, and media attention. There may be a long delay between the death and being able to hold the funeral service. The bereaved's family, their social world, their support systems are all affected. There is likely to be more anger and grief than at other kinds of life-ends. Be kind.

Part 2: Practical guide to arranging a funeral or memorial service

A funeral is the ceremonial marking by those still living of the passing of an era. It is a rite of passage that affirms that a good life is grieved. Many choices will depend on the cultural and religious or secular background of the deceased. Funerals are not only, alas, for the elderly. Stillbirths, SIDS deaths, suicides, traffic accidents, the young... All of these may require special thought and care.

One third of Australians claim no religion, and interesting alternatives to traditional funerals are emerging. It can be helpful to involve family members in the planning. Everyone is comforted by knowing they have been consulted or informed.

Inform closest family and friends by telephone. You can be brief, you can ask someone to do it for you, but it is kind to let those closest know in person. A current issue with social media is that once the information becomes known many will start posting the death (OMG! OMG! Facebook, Twitter, Instagram etc). This can mean that people, especially those in a different time zone, may first hear of the news on their mobile phone, which can cause deep offence. Ask anyone likely to pass on the news this way not to do so until there has been a chance to notify people yourself. Remember, secondly, to inform older or sick friends of the deceased and distant cousins, great-aunts and the like, who can easily slip your mind in this moment of stress.

DEATH NOTICE

Put a notice in the newspaper and also online to notify people of the death. Put in details of the funeral (time and place) or say 'details to follow' if you need time to make arrangements. Do not include details of the wake (to avoid freeloaders). Many people say: 'Donation to such-and-such charity in lieu of flowers'.

> NOTE: If a death is sudden or unexpected the prime mourner may not be available to make contact with others – he or she may be at the hospital, the police station or the coroner's for identification.

A funeral needs almost as much organisation as a wedding, but the organising has to be fitted into only a few days.

SPECIAL INSTRUCTIONS

Check in case the deceased has left special instructions for their funeral. Read the Will, or ring the solicitor if the Will is lodged there, to check whether it contains instructions for the funeral. These wishes should be paramount. Did they wish to donate their organs? Their body to any medical establishment? It is their funeral and no-one else's, but family expectations and traditions will also need to be taken into account.

Decide what type of service is needed. Religious or civil celebrant? Funeral home or church/synagogue/mosque. At home? The beach? Almost anything is allowed as long as it is legal. There are many kinds of death, and this may affect the type of service, the sort of funeral that is needed. The death of a child, a stillbirth, a young person by overdose or road accident[29] may require different choices to someone who has died after a long, good life.

---

29 A quarter of people killed on the roads are under 25

VENUE

Consult your chosen venue about available dates. If overseas family wish to attend, the date of the funeral will have to take into account their arrival dates. If they are unable to come, tell them their apologies will be noted at the funeral.

FUNERAL OR MEMORIAL SERVICE?

You may choose a funeral (with the coffin present) or a memorial service, where the coffin has already been taken to the crematorium, perhaps after a small family service. Often called a 'Celebration of the Life of ...' this can include the wider family, friends and colleagues. Choose family or friends to give the readings and the personal tributes.

In rural situations it is often possible to bury a coffin next to the church, in which case the mourners can gather round for the final committal. In cities, where cemeteries are mostly distant, on the outskirts, the coffin can be driven off to the cemetery or crematorium and the family can continue on to the wake attend the cemetery or crematorium for a small private service at a later time, the next day perhaps. This choice will enable the family to benefit from the important comfort of the wake.

CHILDREN

It is important to talk plainly to children about the situation. Use direct language. No euphemisms such as 'he's gone to sleep', 'he's slipped away into another room', plainly so untrue. An undertaker told me that he had lost his own wife when his four children were aged from five to thirteen. The children took part in helping the nurses, looking after their mother as she sickened. Nothing was hidden from them. They have grown up with no apparent scars, he was glad to say.

By contrast, in the 1920s, my father at age 11 was sent back from prep school and without warning went into his mother's bedroom. She was near death and did not recognise him. He, remembering, said *'Mummy, I didn't know you were sick'*. A few days later he and his brother were sent to play football. As they ran around, they came across a funeral procession. It was his mother's. He had not even been told she had died. He has only mentioned it twice, and each time his voice went up into the uncertain wobble of the devastated small boy he then was. His family probably thought they were protecting him, but I find it hard to forgive people who could be so cruelly thoughtless.

ORDERS OF SERVICE AND SEATING

If you expect a big gathering these may need to be printed, the funeral company will usually do this. If you print it yourself, remember to allocate someone to collect them from the printers. You need to include the names of the priest or celebrant, the names of people giving tributes as well as the hymns and readings. If you are having a wake, include at the end the time, place, and that people are welcome. You may need to omit names of speakers off the order of service if there is uncertainty about who will speak.

Seating for the family needs to be set aside, and a reserved notice put on those rows. The funeral director's staff will hand out the orders of service as people arrive, but you may prefer to ask younger family members to hand them out, to recognise and greet family, special people, and show them to the reserved seats.

EULOGY

A eulogy is a tribute to a person's character. It is not a 'life story' of the person. Sometimes the personality of the deceased is best celebrated through humour and funny stories, but it is not always funny to be funny at a funeral, or unduly tearful. I have been to too many funerals where the young, not having been to any funerals themselves, treat the eulogy as a 'roast', greatly to the distress of the older generation. Mr Davies says the advice he gives about funerals is to make sure the *person in the box* isn't so annoyed that he or she gets out and complains!

It is customary to speak well of the dead, whether they deserve it or not. It can sometimes be a spectator sport to sit and listen as the euphemisms and the omissions roll spoken and unspoken around the gathering.

I have been to two funerals where the deceased was not mourned, where no one seemed to be sorry they had gone. In their way they were sadder than a sad funeral where a good life, one that will leave an apparently irreplaceable gap, is celebrated. A vicar told me that the most distressing funeral he had ever conducted was for a young drug addict in a country town where there had not been a single mourner. Had that neglect been the cause of the young person's drug addiction or was it the result of it? He never knew.

Once a daughter asked if she might speak. She stood next to the coffin and began: 'Father ... I forgive you ...' The whole church seemed to gasp as one. She was very obviously ostracised later at the wake, but if the people present had known how unkindly the widely-loved local doctor we were burying had treated his own family, they would have been more forgiving. One daughter had been driven to suicide. He had refused to help with the education of his grandchildren who he referred to, within their hearing, as 'nothing but little bush rats...'. His daughter deserved her say, and I only hope it helped her come to terms with the lifetime of distress she had borne.

I have said to my children that if, *when* I die, they are sorry I know I will have been a good mother and led a good life (...and I'll be watching!).

MUSIC AND READINGS

It is always lovely to have organ music or a choir at funerals, but this can be expensive. Some religious venues do not allow secular music. Grandchildren may think the latest pop-song is appropriate whereas granny might have preferred Vera Lynn's 'We'll meet again, don't know where don't know when!'.

The most popular music at funerals in the United Kingdom is *Monty Python's* 'Always look on the bright side of life'. In Australia it is currently, 'Wind beneath my wings' and 'Time to say goodbye'. For Christian funerals the 23rd Psalm 'The Lord's my shepherd' and

'Abide with me fast falls the eventide' is often chosen, as is 'I Vow to thee my country'. The most frequently chosen reading is Ecclesiastes 3:1-8[30]; or Timothy 4: 6-8[31].

Another favourite is the traditional Gaelic blessing:
May the road rise up to meet you
May the wind be always at your back
May the sun shine warm upon your face...

Be thoughtful about readings. A poem, written by the young person we were farewelling was read at his funeral. It was beautiful, clever. He had been talented, loved, but the poem showed the turmoil, the unhappiness that had preceded his death. It was a cry for help from the grave. I don't think I was the only person who sat and shivered.

PALLBEARERS

Coffins are mostly taken to the hearse using a wheeled trolley provided by the funeral director, the main mourners walking behind it as it exits after the service. If male relatives wish to carry the coffin themselves, practise beforehand so their shoulder heights slope carefully.

MEMORY STICKS, CDS, DVDS

Be careful. Check before the service. Too often it is discovered immediately before the service that the technology is not compatible. Make an appointment to visit; others may be holding a funeral in the venue.

MEMORIAL BOOK

Most funeral homes provide a book of remembrance to be signed by those attending as part of their service.

---

[30] *'To everything there is a season, a time to be born, and a time to die.'*
[31] *'The time of my departure has come. I have fought the good fight. I have finished the race.'*

FLOWERS FOR THE CASKET

Christian funerals often include flowers, symbolic of growth and regeneration. These are not essential and are not always part of other religions. For a church funeral you need to organise these yourself. Some funeral homes will provide them. Enquire. Take care that in the heat of the moment when nothing, *nothing* seems to be too much for the dear departed, that you do not go over the top. I went over the top. (A daughter, reading this, commented: 'OTT to the max! And wasn't it glorious!').

I heard of a man who loved his veggie patch, and left instructions for his coffin to be covered with red peppers and cabbage leaves. Apparently, it looked magnificent. You can ask the funeral director to deliver the flowers to your home after the funeral, or to a hospital or nursing home. Some people drape a flag over the casket, or place memorabilia such as medals on top.

DRESSING FOR A FUNERAL

Sombre is best. An old friend, a famous florist, died. He had been celebrated for his brilliantly joyous arrangements, so I went dressed in the brightest, most vivid colours I could find. Not one other soul in the whole church was not in the deepest black. I stood out like a tasteless bouquet. He would have adored the drama of the black. I did not dare go on to the wake... I slunk off.

THE WAKE

A wake is a time-honoured tradition. It is supposed to provide 'closure'. However much you feel you cannot face such an event, it is an important part of the farewell. More distant relatives will attend a funeral (open to all) than attend a wedding (by invitation only). It is a chance for them and for old friends to recount family histories and memories of times past. Dear friends need to share the moment. As do work friends, unknown to you perhaps, who want to tell you how greatly they will miss the one you have loved so much. There may even be the odd interloper, suddenly claiming close friendship (and another glass of wine), where no friendship has been known or suspected before, to be quietly avoided. It comforted me to see that my children's friends came to ours to give them support and to see that each had a kind, functioning network around them.

Sometimes it is not easy to decide if you should go on to a wake. You may have known the deceased well, but the after-gathering may be intended mainly for the extended family. If you find you have made the wrong decision, have one drink and then quietly leave. People usually stand around after a funeral and it may be possible to gauge if you are welcome.

In cases of traumatic death, car crash or suicide, the family may wish to gather together privately. If there is dissention in the family it may be better not to hold a wake immediately after the service but perhaps at a later date by invitation only in a private venue, possibly with a slide show of the life being celebrated. This is a good solution if there are people whom the family might like to exclude – after family rifts or the like.

CATERING

Funeral homes and churches usually have a hall and a catering group. Make sure there are chairs available for the elderly. If expense is a concern, choose a morning funeral and keep the food simple – sandwiches, cake, biscuits, tea, coffee – but enough so that people, perhaps having come from a distance, can stay and talk.

Many funeral homes will not allow alcohol to be served. If it is offered, you can ask the serving staff to stop serving alcohol at a certain time if expense is an issue. A dram of whisky is acceptable, but I personally feel that sparkling wine, with its' celebratory overtones, should not be served at a funeral. (Unless, I suppose, you have just inherited the deceased's millions and never liked him in the first place.) You can invite people to your home, but you are unlikely to be in a state to face the organisation. You may have a relative who can help if the gathering is not expected to be large.

THE EVENING AFTER A FUNERAL

The funeral and wake will be draining, but if you suspect that family members may want to return to your home afterwards for an evening meal, give a thought to simple catering. Frozen cakes that can be quickly thawed, drinks, easy finger food (frozen pizzas), barbecue or order a take-away. Delegate firmly. If you find cooking a solace, stock up the fridge. A happy (even if tearful) hugger-mugger of loved ones and helpers in the kitchen can be a most cheering end to such an occasion. You can – and you are allowed to – collapse the next day.

CHAPTER SIX

After a funeral – clearing up

If you are given lemons – make lemonade.

~Traditional Proverb, southern United States

Dealing with end-of-life matters falls into two parts: those that affect the people left, and those that relate to the life and the possessions of the deceased.

FAMILY MEMBERS AND CHILDREN

However shattered you are, there may be others around you who need your immediate care – children who are bewildered or bereft elderly who need comforting. You may be at the centre of a circle of sufferers and need to give sympathy just while you are most in need of it yourself. There is a beautiful book, *Beginnings and Endings with Lifetimes in Between* by Mellonie & Ingpen that explains death clearly in a way that small children can understand. Schools are most helpful at a time like this. It may help for a child to tell their classmates what has happened to them, or it may be preferable for a teacher to do so on their behalf.

If a source of love and care has gone, children need to feel there is still someone who loves them and will look after them. The aftermath of a death is busy, but make sure to take time to sit down and cuddle and talk. You may be lucky to have good support from friends, siblings.

ACKNOWLEDGING LETTERS AND FLOWERS

Many people send flowers as an expression of regret. When I want to send flowers on such occasions, I now send an email or letter to say that they are coming but also that I have asked for them to be delivered in three weeks' time. That is about the time when the first rush of flowers has faded, and new and fresh ones are most welcome.

Letters and flowers may flood in, and some people find acknowledging them can be a burden. I try to avoid sending emails on such an occasion as I feel that an email, though seemingly quick and efficient, can be forgotten in the midst of the drama and is not as comforting as a letter, a concrete (so to speak) thing that can be handled, re-read, put aside and returned to, filed, read again, shared and come across – with pleasure – later. But an email is now the accepted way most of us communicate so ignore me and send one.

Initiate a system to spare yourself the worry about whether you have or have not answered, acknowledged, or noticed letters or kindnesses. I found I was very forgetful in the weeks after our funerals, and it was most helpful to be able to check if I had or had not done something.

Read letters as they arrive. Record each sender, each email and those who sent flowers. Put the letters into a box file. When you write to thank, take five of them out at a time (it is customary to write a thank-you for each condolence letter) *ticking each one off your list* and putting a corresponding tick on each letter. I put aside the special letters, the ones that described how much the dear departed had been valued, those from family, or people of particular interest, and also those that were particularly well written.

One evening we passed those letters round over dinner and we all loved the memories they prompted. I had included some that were clumsily written, trite and impersonal and it was interesting that these were noticed. It was a lesson in letter writing! I have decided that there is great comfort in a thoughtfully composed letter, and they can be preserved and read and re-read a hundred years from now. It is good if their sentiments echo well down the centuries.

Some people like to print a small card to send their thanks. This makes the job much quicker, but I found – however hard and slow it was to answer them all – that I obtained comfort from writing to each dear, kind friend and even to each unknown person who had taken the trouble to write.

PHONE CALLS

It is good to ring to show you care, but never say to a recently bereaved friend 'If there is anything I can do give me a ring'. They won't. After a while, when their life has settled, why not ring and say, 'Next week, Tuesday or Wednesday can I collect you and take you for lunch?', or 'Next Thursday/Friday we are coming to help you with… the shopping, the garden (or whatever)'. Your friend can say no, but they will not have to take the initiative.

LIFE AFTER LOSS

If you have had a long vigil, you may have neglected yourself and it can be sensible to have a check-up.

THINGS THAT NEED ATTENTION AFTER A DEATH

The Council for the Aging (COTA) has a thirty-two-page checklist that is very useful.[32] It sets out everything that you may need to think of after a death.

Return hired equipment, walking frames, wheelchairs, and other pieces.

---

32   www.cotavic.org.au

You may need to notify a number of people/organisations. Here is a short checklist (not a comprehensive list):

- employer
- health professionals (doctor, dentist, physiotherapist),
- priest
- landlord
- bank/credit union
- superannuation
- Centrelink (pension) or Department of Veteran's Affairs (pension)
- local council.
- health fund
- insurance (life, house, car)
- accountant
- services and utilities: electricity, gas, telephone/internet, water, post office (PO box), newsagent, trade union, clubs and associations.

A car cannot be owned by a dead person. Notify your licensing authority, and if you do so within two weeks of the owner's death you will get a refund of the licence fee. You will need to transfer ownership of the car.

APPLYING FOR PROBATE

You need to apply to the Supreme Court in your area and print an application form on their website. It is not necessary to put one in a newspaper as in the past.

You must include the full name of the deceased, all executors, and a contact address for each executor. This is done in case anyone has reason to challenge the will. For instance, a later Will may have been written or different executors chosen. Distribution cannot begin until probate has been granted.

Probate is not needed for small estates – $15,000NZ dollars cash-in-bank, and I am told $85,000AUD in Australia.

You can download do-it-yourself forms.[33]

OBTAINING PROBATE

Sometimes called a grant of representation, this is a critical step that certifies that the Will is valid and it confirms the appointment of the executor. Without it the executor does not have the authority to administer the estate or transfer assets. Bank accounts etc., will be closed until probate is granted, and until then they cannot be accessed by anyone one not authorised to do so. If there is no Will (person dies intestate) it is necessary to apply for a letter of administration.[34]

FINANCIAL AFFAIRS

After a huge change in your circumstances – whether death, divorce or a change in health – it is essential to quickly take stock. You may be tired, scatty, confused. You will probably tell yourself you are coping. But take care and start by facing the cool, cruel, unpalatable (perhaps) facts.

FINANCIAL ADVICE

If a death has made a change in your circumstances, you may find you have less money than is comfortable or, if you are lucky, more than you are used to looking after. Sit down, look at the information you have, and see if it makes sense to you. You may have a financial adviser who can help you understand exactly what your position is. Listen to what they say and keep notes. Don't necessarily listen to friends and family.

Two weeks later, look at the information again. Are you going to be able to make sense of it? Do you understand it? If not, go back and listen to the professional advice again. Don't be embarrassed that you might sound silly if you ask the same question again… and again. You would be far more stupid if you did not!

---

33   www.aussielegal.com.au
34   www.hocw.com.au is a good website that clearly explains Grants of Representation

MAKE NO DECISIONS IN THE HEAT OF THE MOMENT

Do not make big decisions or let yourself be pressured to make decisions immediately after a loss. Take care. First, survive the initial shock. Then slowly put your new life together. Remember this is a *new* life and this time you are in charge.

Do you want to remain where you are living? Are you able to do so financially? You may need to apply to Centrelink for income support. The local council can mostly be relied upon for sympathetic advice. Are you able to cope on your own? You may be surrounded by kindly, well-intentioned advice. Listen to it, and remember it, but do nothing major (such as selling your house) until you are in a calm frame of mind and can think clearly. You will think you can 'get a grip of yourself' and that you are in a state to be decisive and able to make sensible decisions, but I have seen enough people decide, quickly and disastrously, that I say again: *wait*.

Immediately following her husband's funeral, I heard that a friend's house had been put on the market. I was concerned. I knew her garden was the other half of her soul: a source of solace, fascination, exercise, a place of dedicated peace and... food.

The garden, though not large, held a hundred different edible plants, she told everyone proudly. There were apples, pears, plums, nuts, vines, bushes, berries, herbs, tomatoes. And rows of small things in all colours: carrots, beets, squads of neat greens. She ate, she bottled, she gave away the produce. She said her children had thought it would be too much for her on her own. The inside of the house was similarly encrusted with joyous, loved objects. She has a balcony now. Her voice trails off as she tells you that she can't get out on to it... for the plants. I am sure her mourning was doubled with both her husband and her garden gone.

SORTING DOCUMENTS AND PAPERS AFTER A DEATH

Sort. Keep. Give. Digitise. *Chuck!*

Keep necessary financial records/property titles, business documents, etc., plus invoices for significant purchases such as artworks (not sofas and the like). Remember, when sorting out bank statements, share transactions papers, financial, information, that the Tax Office requires you to keep records for seven years. Banks now keep such records only for two years. If you require older records, they can still access them, but with some delay.

Keep family records (birth, marriage, death certificates), personal papers of interest to the family (prizes, military records, family letters).

The executor will know which chattels, furniture, and other goods are not covered by the Will. Have a family discussion about what to keep. These can be offered round to family members, sent to auction or put on eBay (a younger member of the family might have fun with this). Buy coloured stickers to mark possessions, for example: blue = Susie, green = Richard, red = keep, yellow = throw, white = instructions for disposal.

Small items can be given as keepsakes. Do not stress. No hurry. But when you feel you can face it, dispose of clothes, shoes, bags to op-shops, vintage clothing shops. Books can go to second-hand bookstores. Charities such as The Brotherhood of St Lawrence make money on eBay from the old books they are given.

HIDDEN OR LOST?

Look out for the unexpected. Was the deceased in the habit of hiding cash around their home where no burglar (or you) could ever find it? In a hollowed-out book? A tin in the refrigerator? Coffee tin? Freezer? Did they hide their jewellery among their underwear, in the butter container, or taped under the lid of the garbage bin? (Don't laugh – it's been done). A woman bought a battered old suitcase at the sale of Agatha Christie's possessions after her death for £20, on opening, she found it contained all Agatha Christie's jewellery.

PERSONAL PAPERS

I have learned the hard way that it is not efficient to keep everything, however neatly filed. Sooner or later someone, even if not yourself, will need to dispose of them.

As people get sick they do not often accept that *'now!'* is a better time to do things than *'when I feel better'*. It is a frequent comment from those clearing up after a death which occurred following a long illness that when drawers and filing cabinets are opened, piles of unpaid bills and correspondence, matters on which action was imperative, can be discovered unopened.

Two people I know keep everything – they have both led fascinating and busy lives. But their papers! You walk down their entrance halls and there are stacks of papers, tall, stiff, like grenadier guards watching as you pass. There are piles up the stairs (one owner is doddery – the piles would be terrifying to slip on), piles on sofas, round the sides of rooms, kitchen chairs, the dresser. Each kitchen has one seat, only, that is free (the owner's) to be sat on. It's useless to expect to be able to sit down if you are offered a coffee! One thinks with deep pity for the people left with the clearing up – the piles would take a lifetime to sort and so, alas, items of historic importance will most likely be chucked out with the rest.

I was invited, once, into another house. There was a path to walk, single file, through stacks of forty? fifty? years of newspapers piled shoulder high in columns that covered the living room through to the kitchen at the back. The owner was kind and mentally sharp, but I do not fancy his chances if there happened to be a fire! I also shudder at the problem when he goes. (Bobcat?)

SORTING A LOVED ONE'S BELONGINGS

It is easy to know what should be done, but sometimes very hard to actually do. Possessions, *things* can have a life of their own. Objects can speak of the person gone, sometimes of a life unsuspected or of interests shared and unshared. Someone went to clear his long-divorced wife's house after her death and found that beside her bed she had exactly the same pile of books that were just then beside his. He suffered a wave of grief – a loss, redoubled, of all that they had not shared over the years.

In my house I was slow at dealing with the clothes and wish I had tackled them sooner. It was a great emotional difficulty. If dealt with quickly, it feels as if you are trampling on a grave. If left, the moth might get there faster than the needy to whom they could prove a blessing. They all had so many memories attached. Open the wardrobe and it seems that there is someone still living there. Shoes, especially, seem to ooze personality (and *noise*... you can almost hear them walking). Discarding them felt like throwing my husband out in person, but it is a problem that does not go away until faced. The local op-shop greeted each armful with a glad smile. Check the pockets and the lapels for contents. I discovered that old formal clothes which did not fit anyone in our family were particularly welcome and that they are apparently loved by the young.

My husband had not been a handyman. Faced with any small maintenance he had always come back, glowing with pride, with the new hammer, saw, pliers that were perfect for the job. Nails, he knew, were more economical by the pillow than by the packet. We had sacks of nuts, tacks, short nails, long nails, longer nails, zinc coated long nails. We had short screws, long screws, plain and some brass-coated. We had many hammers, a lot of saws and files, screwdrivers by the dozen and... pliers! The jobs would remain undone, but we had a happy father/husband. But oh! The problem of getting rid of several tons, it seemed, of such things after he died. All we could do as we carried them in relays to the bin was laugh ruefully. (We should have thought of the nearest Men's Shed.).

He also loved music or thought he did. He would come in beaming happily with new sets of concertos, requiems, the complete works of his favourite composers. He would never actually play them. They are not to my taste. I like the human voice, anything melodic, sung: acapella to zydeko. I say to myself that I should at least play his CDs before I give them away, but they sit there still, happily wrapped in their cellophane, too 'good' to... *Chuck!*

If I gently poke fun at his *'little ways'*, it is only because I remember with gratitude how patient (he might have said long-suffering) he was about mine. We were both tolerant of the other's 'little ways' but looking back I wish I had given him a birthday present along the lines of 'buy no more CDs and in exchange tell me three of my habits you find trying and I will try to change!'

Nigel had kept every tiny, small letter from the whole of his life, it seemed, dating back from when he was at school, far too many to sort with care. They were a nuisance but easy to deal with. We digitised some that appeared of interest, then... *Chuck!*

The same had happened when my mother-in-law died. She had been a doctor, brilliant of intellect, ferocious of temper. She had had a very interesting life and had kept up a copious correspondence worldwide. Once, ruefully, she said she expected we would throw them away when she died. She was right. The letters, mostly handwritten in fading inks, with the various scrawls creeping illegibly across varying colours and shapes of paper, had all been kept in big envelopes that seemed to explode everywhere once opened. The same... *Chuck!* Which was perhaps a pity. At the time she died we had been overwhelmed with our own burgeoning families and had not the time to sort through them. I tell you this because if only she had kept less of them, a selection, we might have read them and enjoyed them.

Alas, it was a lesson. If you keep *everything* it is too, too much for anyone to thoughtfully sort out. I keep separate files on segments of my life that contain facts and records that I may need to refer to, but which can be disposed of when I die. I have one, different, file called 'Mum – Nice Things' in which I keep the nicest letters, the memories, articles I have written, the sort of things that make me flutter with pleasure or interest every time I peep into it. It bulges but it is not so large that perhaps after me my children may enjoy reading through some of it before... *Chuck!*

This reminds me of one more job I need to do. As I write I make a note to myself to clean out my cupboards. I did so a year before, and the year before that. But I must, I really must. If I do not do so, it will be a hideous job for someone else, and it is not kind to leave problems behind so that someone else in their busy life has to expend the sort of energy on what you have not found time, in your busy life, to spend. I was recently tempted to buy myself another filing cabinet, but then decided it was better to sort out *(Chuck!)* my present one to make room for the things I wanted to add.

GRIEF COUNSELLOR

(my personal experience)

One day, about three years after Nigel's death, I broke out in a most uncharacteristic fury at a family meeting. We were all startled, most of all me. Oh! The difficulty of solving problems when the background has been lost. There was a matter that I felt would have taken only a second for him to deal with but was a nightmare in terms of time and dead-ends for us to solve.

The next day a resourceful daughter handed me a piece of paper 'Grief counsellor' it said. I refused, feeling cross again. How could anyone help? How could anyone else know the aggravation of it? Of course, I would not benefit from some unknown, well-meaning 'expert'. How could anyone be an 'expert' in my problems? However, after much gentle persuasion, I rang.

A kind, patient, non-judgemental and very professional lady took down various details. I explained my unfortunate burst of anger. "Widowed three years?" she said – it's normal. She told me that buried resentments can surface sometime afterwards. It was extraordinary. The moment I was told *"It's normal"*, I was free to deal both with my anger and the problems that caused it.

I had not realised that I still needed help. After all, it was years after the event, and I thought I had faced and solved everything I needed to face and solve. I was amazed to find that the cool judgement of an impersonal, professional ear could prove so utterly invaluable.

This kind and professional lady explained that she would keep my details for six weeks, and that she would not contact me but that I was welcome to come and see her if I felt the need. She sounded as if she really meant it, and I wish I could go back and thank her. But the affirmation that someone else thought I had reason to be angry, and that it was a quite normal and common reaction, liberated me. I felt no need to go, but that does not mean it would not be helpful to you.

Remember that if you find you are in distress, get help. Professional advisers are just that: professional. They have seen it all before. They are dispassionate, they take the 'personal' out of a personal situation. They do not gossip. What is new to you is commonplace to them. It helps to put your unique problem where it belongs – amongst the problems that we all – every one of us – have sooner or later to find our way through. But, if a coffee with your best friend has not helped, it can be amazingly comforting to have a cool, well-judged, helping hand who has seen it all before, and will help you face up to your problems, to deal with or find ways around them.

A daughter commented on reading this that she thought the above counselling advice – while great – was slightly hypocritical. "You didn't follow any of your own advice despite us all urging you to do so," she said. Oh well. If I went through it all again, I would do so.

To be been widowed after a long and happy marriage is not the worst you can suffer. I always weep for the women I see on the news who have lost a husband – perhaps a fire-fighter, a soldier, a policeman. They have, too often, a couple of small, bewildered children clutched by their side and no doubt a hefty mortgage. They won't have the privilege of being tired for a year. They will have to pull themselves together to support their children and go straight back to work.

I often come across delightful middle-aged women who have not married, who grieve that they have not found a partner, had children. To them, a person who has had that love and companionship has been lucky beyond measure. To them, widowhood is a safe, lucky, companionable, enviable state – a respectable, comfortable port. It is a demonstration that you have once been loved.

CHAPTER SEVEN

Facing a new life

*Two men look out from prison bars,
one sees mud and the other sees stars.*

~Dale Carnegie

*Remember to look up at the stars and not down at your feet.
Try to make sense of what you see and wonder
about what makes the universe exist. Be curious.
And however difficult life may seem,
there is always something you can do and succeed at.
It matters that you don't just give up.*

~Professor Stephen Hawking

THE INITIAL SHOCK AFTER LOSS

There is no right way to mourn. Every mourning is different. One person may be despairing, desolate. Another may be relieved that someone is free from the pain, the indignities of a slow death. Or just glad. Perhaps the deceased had been a bully, a drinker or heavily, exhaustingly dependent.

Enraged. Jubilant or relieved, not everyone has loved a dead one.

Do not underestimate the effect of a bereavement or a deep shock on you, because the effects are powerful. A medical practitioner told me there can be actual physiological changes in people due to grief. Grief you do expect, but recurring melancholy can also haunt your life. Melancholy is as treacherous as black ice on a freezing day – you find yourself sliding on it suddenly, unexpectedly. Take care, you can slip easily from grief to depression, and that will then be yet another problem that you will need to tackle.

Survive the initial shock. Whatever is right for you is right and normal for you. It's OK to feel exhausted, miserable, wrecked. It's OK to feel elated. Feel whatever you need to feel. Then slowly put your new life together.

I am sure we do not all cope with loss the same way. I spent a time in my early teens living in a remote house. My sister was much younger, my brother was a baby. Our milk came every morning in a herd of goats, the climate was hot and so school ended at 1 o'clock. I have come to realise that I learnt how to be happy spending a great deal of time in my own company, and that this has stood me in good stead at this latter part of my life.

I lived my life the other side of the world from my mother, who was a serene, unshakable source of love and understanding to me. Now passed, she is only a little less absent to me than she was for most of my life. I feel I can put out my hand and still be comforted by her wisdom and kindness. But I found, also, that I was left with a deep guilt that my life-choice had resulted in her grandchildren being distant, and myself, her daughter, not being part of her life. Friends whose mothers lived nearby seem to mourn more the immediate things – their mother's smile, the babysitting, mending, the advice, the *involvement* in their life. It may be that if a person has had unbroken family support and closeness their whole lives, that losing a such a person might be a much greater shock to their everyday life.

It is worthwhile to remember that one half of every couple – whether from divorce or death – has to tackle the future on their own. Tell yourself that you can do it. Remind yourself how often you have re-invented yourself already, how many 'skins' you have shed like a lizard along the way: being an outsider at a new school, trying to be a sophisticated, smart party animal, a responsible career person, the perfect new 'other half'. Being the parent of a teenager (that was a hard one to get right!), or responsible, impartial referee of family disputes. At each stage you found a new persona, you were the person you needed to be at the time.

Now you are alone, needing to reinvent yourself once more, but this time, tell yourself that at least you have had practise at altering yourself, and your life, to changed circumstances.

Everyone faces different deaths. But Ann Tyler, the famous novelist (If Morning Ever Comes) faced something very much like the death I faced. When I read her account, I found myself moved to tears – someone else knew what it felt like....

Ann was married to a child psychiatrist who was sick with cancer for three years and, like my husband, would not admit that he could, or would, die. She said she wishes they could have had one conversation about it. "It's as if I went through his death alone," she said. When he died, she had a rule that she had to have one human contact every day, otherwise she never would have left the house. She says she remembers thinking "Does visiting the dentist count?".

It can be a great comfort to know that others find life – and living – hard. I would love to think that you might get the same comfort from reading my story as I did reading Ann Tyler's account.

COMPLICATED GRIEF

Sometimes, especially with a suicide or the death of a child, time does not cure. When a person cannot recover it is a separate, deep problem, and professional help should be sought. *Beyond Blue* is a good place to begin.

ANNIVERSARIES

Anniversaries and commemorations can be healing, a reason for a family and friends to gather with a common purpose to share good – and sad – memories. In cases of trauma – car accidents, suicides – the occasion might only serve to foster recriminations, distress. Be selfish about this. Make sure those around you know what is helpful for you at this time.

Myself, I cannot bear to have any recognition of the anniversary of my husband's death. I tell you my story in this book, but the way he died was so distressing to me that I cannot bear to think of it or to be reminded of it. I spend the day alone. But, strangely, I have noticed that it just so happens that – quite coincidentally – a child seems always to invite their family to dinner every year on that day. We talk about the lost, loved father but we do not refer to the fact it is a special day. The kindness behind that gentle acceptance of my distress is more valuable to me than anything else I could ever imagine.

Difference

How powerful a presence is her absence:
No Sheba naps, curled on the counterpane,
Of sits by the window to memorize the rain,
Or tussles with the tassels of a valance
With tigress energy and murderous talons,
Or attends with steady gaze the slow routine
Of household duties droning round again
From her vigilant bookshelf eminence.

The armchair seems not empty but incomplete
And the patch of sunlit rug unoccupied
More vacant than the sky when the moon is hid
In the cavern of December's longest night.
The rooms were quiet when she was resident.
Now they lie silent. That is different.

~Fred Chappell

THE SILENCE – THE FIRST SHOCK OF BEING ALONE

Shortly after a loss, the *other* most dreadful moment suddenly occurs. The family, the friends have left, the flowers have faded. You suddenly have less to do; no visits, no nursing. Your parent, your partner, your love, your child or the traitorous oaf has gone forever. You finally understand how deeply, utterly emotionally drained you are. You walk into your house, or their house, your kitchen, or their kitchen, and you suddenly feel *the silence.*

Some silences are quieter than others, have you noticed? This one seems to roll around your life like thunder. You drop a fork. It tinkles... the tinkle echoes. You turn to the sink and feel you have bumped into silence as if it is a real, solid body like a childhood ogre waiting to grab you. It feels malign, cold. You feel like saying 'excuse me' and stepping round it. There was silence before, remember? There was quietness before, but there *was* always the possibility of approaching footsteps, of a book dropping, a car door slamming, a paper rustling in the corner, a clearing of the throat hoping you might think of making coffee.

Even now, if I look up quickly, I swear I can see the back of his head in his favourite chair. It is eerie walking up the stairs to bed... and finding the bed is empty. You wake in the night. There is no quiet breathing (snoring) beside you. It is too quiet to sleep. Now, many years later when I wake, I feel wrapped in the warmth of my memories. I reach over, turn on the radio – I am not disturbing anyone – and I lie there happy. It does happen.

Understand that this terrifying, unaccustomed silence will, gradually, morph into a gentle peace, and a welcome friend walking in your door will sound like an elephant invading in tap shoes!

It is interesting that some people seem to have a time of day when they feel worst. A family was so concerned that their mother could not bear the time each evening when her husband had always walked through the door, that they encouraged her to go to her local club to play the pokies, to meet and see people. It was not until they found that she had gambled her entire house away that they understood what a mistake this had been.

Take stock of your life: what can help when your world is changed

It matters not how straight the gate,
How charged with punishment the scroll.
I am the master of my fate,
I am the captain of my soul.

~William Ernest Henley

It is most important that you do not do anything major, drastic with your life for about twelve months after a major bereavement. You will be emotionally vulnerable to helpful (or self-serving) suggestions from those around you. You may make mistakes to make a problem go away or to simplify your life that you will regret when you are in a calmer frame of mind.

NEEDS AND WANTS

It is important to differentiate between what you *need* – often little – and what you *want* – quite often a lot. It is possible to live with compromise.

Grief is a universal experience, but every grief is complex and unique. It differs from person to person but surviving it can be greatly shaped by our attitude. One thing is certain: if you expect life to be 100% happy, you will end up 100% disappointed. If you expect to be 50% happy you will end up deeply thankful that things are not 50% worse!

It is good to take stock of your life at any time, but this is the Great Divide. This is the Red Sea in your life, the time you make it across to unexplored territory and strike out into a different world. If, as Leonard Cohen put it, you find yourself 'sliding down the razor blade of life' decide carefully what sort of life you want to live and what qualities you need to survive and enjoy your new life.

It is important to keep on with some of the comforting old routines, but it is also important to put a different framework around parts of your life, to feel you have a new life with interesting possibilities rather than the old one with losses and sadnesses inbuilt. Your life will not stop, even if you think it has just done so.

Many partnerships are unevenly entwined. One side may have set the main 'tone' – his friends were their friends, or she organised their social life, for example. Someone who has nursed a partner though a long illness may find it especially hard to make a new life, but when they do it may include much of what they would have liked to do all along. Haven't been to the theatre for years? Your partner didn't much like films? Go! On your own or with a friend. You will discover to your surprise that life goes on. Television seemed banal after everything I had gone through. We had mostly enjoyed the same programs. Sometimes I had groaned inwardly at his choices, no doubt he was occasionally as patient with mine. After a while I noticed that there is a surprising amount of pleasure to be found in having the remote control firmly in your hand – not to be countermanded! Take note of these small pleasures.

I found it helpful to cut out everything I had kept on from habit such as magazines and activities we had shared. This may be the first time for decades that you can be yourself. You, not 'us'. However wonderful 'us' was, it can be disconcerting to discover that 'me' is still there, still interested, still avid for life.

There were big things that helped, but I found it was often the small everyday things that made me focus on the present, to get through a difficult day, to survive. If you are cooking for one less person, it can be a surprisingly good step to buy yourself smaller cookware. Do not think this is a minor suggestion. My old faithful pans, my friends, were too big for my present reality. Every night I had a depressing reminder that my life was now different – that I was now cooking for one. So I went out and bought a small frying pan with a lid which, like Goldilocks, was not too big and not too small – but was just right.

If you have not been through such a loss you may laugh. You may even sneer. But remembering back I realise that this was a powerful mechanism to help me face my current reality, to accept that my life was now, always, going to be different. That I needed to adapt and that I could take steps to make my life function again. Going to a shop, choosing it, paying for it was all part of accepting that my life had changed, and that I needed to change as well.

I had always hated our knives and forks. They were ugly and uncomfortable to hold. My husband had thought there was nothing wrong with them at all. Sometime after he died, I went out and bought new ones. I enjoyed exploring what was on offer. I chose a modern design which sat well in the hand. The spoons were beautiful.

I was well aware that what I was *actually* buying was an acknowledgement and an acceptance of independence. It was a symbol to me that it was possible that I could act alone, that I could take charge of my life and that it was in my power to make it what I wanted. From that moment I decided that if I made the effort to cope, then I could, I *would* cope.

I am not suggesting that you rush out and buy something! But I *am* suggesting that it can be a surprisingly affirmative step to take a decision – *any* decision – about *anything* independently on your own when you have always before discussed and agreed on a course of action together as a couple.

People are often praised for soldiering on, managing, keeping up an appearance of good cheer. But I have to say, I sometimes found myself longing for the old Victorian custom – mourning – the recognition that a period of deep sadness, of reflection, a re-grouping, is needed.

ALONE OR LONELY?

If you are lonely when you are alone,
you are in bad company.

~Jean-Paul Sartre

Researchers have found that one third of people over 65 live alone, and that divorced or separated men between 45 and 64 have the highest rates of emotional loneliness. Two-fifths of older people say television is their main company. Some people feel they have always been very alone – as a student, or even in their marriage. Grief, however it happens, is a lonely place. People are living longer and family members often live at a distance. The United Kingdom has recently appointed a Minister for Loneliness. It is a large problem worldwide.

It is now thought that one of the secrets to happiness and longevity is seeing people you know and like, daily. Chronic loneliness apparently alters the expression of our genes in every cell of our bodies. And not in a good way. As well, two neuropeptides – oxytocins and vasopressin – are secreted in the bloodstream when we form and maintain meaningful relationships, and these chemicals help to counter stress and repair wounds. Numerous studies show that people with active social lives have higher cancer survival rates than those who are isolated. That does not prove a causal link: the kind of people who have active social lives might also be the kind of people with stronger resistance to cancer, but a study of rats in which the females were randomly separated, some to live in groups and the others in isolation, found that the isolated females developed 84 times the amount of breast cancer tumours as those that were placed in groups.

Neglecting to keep in close contact with people who are important to you is thought to be at least as dangerous to your health as a pack-a-day cigarette habit, hypertension, or obesity. 'Meetings' does not mean Twitter or Instagram but actual, real physical meet-ups.

Loneliness can have significant physical effects making people more prone to trouble sleeping, stomach issues, nausea, infections. Another recent study compared 148 studies of survival after heart attacks. It found that the chances of surviving a heart attack overwhelmingly depends upon the quality of supportive friendships a person has; second only to giving up smoking.

A report recently put out by the Australian Psychological Society and Swinburne University (November 2018) measured loneliness in Australia for the first time. It found that one in four adults are lonely.

So, if you feel lonely just remember... *you are not alone!*

Never forget: you can be alone but not lonely. I am alone but I am not lonely. A large part of my world is within me. I find that I *farm* my memories for the pleasures they give me. The good, the bad, the wonderful and I reap a rich harvest. I believe that no one dies from this world until the last person who remembers them with love, dies also. My husband is still very much alive to me. His body has died but not his spirit. Old friends, my grandmother, who once populated my world have morphed into a comfortable wallpaper of memories that people my inner world. I find I am happy living with this jostling throng of ghosts – as long as I also go out and seize the rest of life with both hands!

But common sense must reign. Sociability should not be yet another health obligation like walking, the latest fad, or not drinking too much.

If you are newly alone you can become withdrawn, or it can have the opposite effect. I find I can be too talkative in company. Did you ever think talking was fun? It never was when you had someone to talk to whenever you liked. But nowadays when I sit down with a friend, I have to be careful to be quiet, to let them get a word in edgeways. I want to hear all about their life, their troubles, their children but I can talk the leg off a donkey if given the chance!

My husband was the sort of man who thought before he spoke. What he then said was worth listening to. I am the sort of person who flies in, adverbs and adjectives jostling with thoughts for ear-room. Some of us try to be perfect, and some of us (me) know we have to try a little harder.

> A hint: When you live alone it is easy to become self-absorbed. Take care, especially, with health as a topic of conversation. For your best friends you willingly listen again and again. And again. And gladly. But, and we have all felt it, sooner or later one feels a little down oneself and thinks one might just put off another meeting with a groaner for a while. Or a long while, perhaps. Germaine Greer is quoted as saying that she allows her friends five minutes for an 'organ recital'. Thereafter health is a forbidden topic. Sensible.

> Another hint: When your life has changed forever, make sure you treasure yourself above all. Avoid things or people who cause you distress. A friend asked me for coffee. She was all care and kind concern. "How are you?" she said, "all *alooone* in that house of yours, don't you feel that you rattle around in it? And *niiight*, how do you manage *all alooooone* at night? Aren't you *afraiiid*, all on your *oooown*?"
>
> "Not until you mentioned it," I said.

I found I was so unsettled by this conversation that if she rings I find I am quite happy if, by chance, I am unable to join her. Disloyal? To her, perhaps, but not to myself. But this is where you need to find courage to take the path that is right for *you*.

> A warning: Take care that you do not close your front door and become *too* self-sufficient. Make sure you also look outwards and go out. If you find yourself happy with your alone-ness (as can happen) never forget the long-term necessity and pleasure of having a presence in the big world outside your small, inner world. In other words: *If you shut your door make sure you leave your windows open – wide!*

The Victorian Government has a program 'Strengthening Seniors Inclusion and Participation in Local Communities initiative', which focuses on the problems of social isolation. There are many Senior Citizens centres which need, and love, volunteers. All states have versions of this program[35]. If you need to: GO!

One of the most surprising things when you are first by yourself, such a small thing you may think, and so strange to remark on, is entering a room alone from which the noises of a happy gathering are coming. It had not worried me since I was shy and young. It can be surprisingly difficult if you are used to a companion at your elbow. I stood outside doors afraid to go in. If this happens to you, as it may, stop for a moment and think. You can slide into that room as 'poor me', or you can straighten your shoulders and enter it as a dignified survivor. You choose.

I chose. It did not make it easier, but gradually it is something you become used to.

Cognitive behavioural therapy is currently judged to be one of the most effective ways of changing your behaviour and thinking and improving your life. There are websites but they are changing so fast. Get up-to-date advice.

---

[35] www.seniorsonline.vic.gov.au/seniors

TRAVELLING ALONE

Travelling alone is hard at first. Take a smaller suitcase, make sure it has wheels, as help is not always at hand. Accommodation is more expensive for one. Restaurants are unavoidable when travelling and a lone person taking up a whole table for one bill is not always made welcome. Instead of raging, tell yourself that you could be a high-powered executive with the United Nations, and it is a rare evening that you have escaped your security detail and you are determined to enjoy every moment of your rare freedom. It works, if for no other reason that the possibility is so outrageous. It can be helpful to have a small book in your handbag to tide you over a long wait.

Over the years I had sometimes dreamed of having a day on my own in some cities. How lovely to slide through the shops, not just for myself, and not only for clothes, you understand. Oh no no, no! Moi? But to be able to choose presents for the children, grandchildren, and friends without being rushed, I told myself. To be sure sometimes Nigel would suddenly wheel me into a dress shop – inevitably the garment that had caught his eye was of the size that I was when we married. I look back and wonder if he always thought of me as that girl, whether he had ever noticed that I had plumped, greyed, wrinkled! But there is no getting past the fact that the real fun of travelling is comparing notes about what you have seen, being amazed at what your partner knows about some obscure corner of the world, swapping ideas, marvelling at the different, the new, the unexpected... *together.*

My children had been the greatest support both to their father and myself over the past few dreadful years. I decided that the best way to thank them was to be as independent as I could manage. I would accept advice about my computer and financial affairs. I promised myself that I would then make every effort not to be a burden. That meant displaying a semblance of good cheer and the appearance of coping. And it is always amazing to me that if you fool all those around you – the most important person you also fool is yourself! You do not fool yourself entirely, of course, but just enough to see that there may be another path you can walk if you just put out your foot to take that first step.

STAY WELL – LOOK AFTER YOURSELF, EAT WELL

That is, don't skimp. Good health is your best ally in life. Too plump? Your knees and feet may go. Too thin? There is nothing to fall back on in times of sickness. Some people hate cooking. So cook simply. Ready-prepared meals are available, and choose nutritious food.

THREE INTERESTING TESTS THAT MAY HELP YOU BEGIN TO FIND THE RIGHT PATH

The 'why do I get out of bed?' test: You may never have needed to ask yourself before, but a doctor told me it is important to have an answer to this apparently simple question: 'What gets you out of bed?' Family? Work? Dog? Friends? The need to look after yourself (shopping, food or laundry)? An interest? Volunteering commitments? You feel well and want to walk? Your answer will put much of your life into context, although it could be grim for those who can't think of a good reason to get up. Nevertheless, soldier on. You may find it gets better as the day goes on.

The 'dark hours' test: After a shock, such as bereavement or a divorce, you will find yourself waking in the dark hours of the night in fright or rage. It is important to ask yourself what distresses you most. The loss? The things unsaid? A change in your circumstances? You trawl over all the fun, the sadnesses, the regrets, the good, the bad. You feel cold. After some time (much time, I have to say) I find that I have reached a peaceful place. I am able to reclaim the good memories from the past because to lose those memories is yet another loss – the loss of the life you've lived.

The A4 test: Take a piece of A4 paper. Draw a line across it halfway down and a line down the middle. In the top left quarter write down three things that are *good* about your life, that you are glad of. In the top right list three things that, *if you could make yourself do them*, would be a source of immense relief to you, a weight off your mind. In the bottom left, list three deep griefs, regrets. In the bottom right write three things that you ought to do but absolutely cannot face. The left side is for emotions, the right side for practical matters. The deceased may feature top left: 'Thank goodness he's gone'; or bottom left: 'total tragedy'. Money might be top right: 'I can manage'; or bottom right" 'Help!'

This is very simple. Put it aside and look at it the next day. You may find it puts much of your life in context if only because you have had to leave out so many of the fluttering, distracting crowd of difficulties that will be jostling for your attention. It makes clearer which urgent, essential problems should take immediate priority.

The same solution does not work for everyone, and what may be helpful at the ages of 30 or 40 may not be of much help if you are 60 or 70. Generally speaking it seems that time is the best of all cures, but that can be a slow journey. I missed my husband, but I also missed having someone to care for, to fuss over, to think of. I was not *needed*.

It may be helpful to think hard about how you want to live your life. I feel most of humanity is good, is kind. Read this little poem, and then look at the date it was written!

> *As each day ends may I have lived,*
> *That I may truly say:*
> *I did no harm to humankind,*
> *From truth I did not stray.*
> *I did no wrong with knowing mind,*
> *From evil did I keep.*
> *I turned no hungry person away,*
> *I caused no one to weep.*

~The Book of the Dead. Ancient Egypt (ca.1600 BC)

RETURNING TO WORK

Not everyone has the luxury of quietly taking stock. Returning to work may be necessary for financial reasons or it may provide a comforting continuity to your life. Most workplaces are understanding. Make sure your co-workers know about your bereavement (perhaps ask a colleague to tell them) so that you do not continually have to repeat yourself, and also make sure your supervisor is aware of the situation. You may be scatty. If so, it is more sensible to have your work checked than to lose a good reputation. Such concerns can be overwhelming at a time like this. Many helpful websites are available. Google 'Returning to work after a Death'.

Be aware that after a death the whole world is changed for those who survive. Samantha Cameron's son Ivan died just before his seventh birthday, the year before his father became Prime Minister of England. She wrote movingly not only about the wrenching grief of losing her son but also of the shock she had felt when the supportive world of doctors, kind nurses and social services that had been of such comfort was suddenly gone as well.

> *There's a crack, a crack in everything*
> *– that's how the light gets in.*
>
> ~Leonard Cohen, Anthem

COPING WITH TIME ON YOUR HANDS

If you have been nurse, companion, cook, chauffeur you can suddenly have a lot of time on your hands – more than you have had for years. If time seems to hang sadly on a hook in the corner, you might like to consider volunteering, on a temporary basis at first, for some good cause. Volunteer groups are made up of caring people who are interested in the world around them. Each of them will have an unexpected story, unusual qualities, a sad loneliness, perhaps, but each will open your eyes to other ways of being. They will all have a different reason for volunteering, it is likely you will find you have more in common that you could ever have imagined. I love watching such groups: there is usually an air of great goodwill. There is always one whom the rest are carrying and another who tests the patience of all. But the smiles speak louder than words.

Eight of us were sitting round coffee one day. I was next to a friend who was always exquisitely groomed, well-read, perceptive, and endlessly cheerful. We were congratulating her on her extraordinarily generous use of her time, the good work she did volunteering for certain worthy, but hard causes. She was looking modestly at the table, and only I heard her say quietly, under her breath, "It gets me out of bed in the morning." I was astonished. Here was someone who had chosen a path that helped herself as much as those she helped. I looked at her with new respect and a great rush of empathy. Courage can come in the quietest and most unexpected packages.

Not long after writing this I stood at a supermarket wearing a silly Father Christmas hat asking for Christmas donations of food for the poor. I began noticing several people who came to shop, left holding one piece of shopping and who returned twice, three, even four times, leaving each time with a single item. I realised that the people I was watching were there for another reason. Shopping can be a friendly, companionable activity, mild exercise, protected from the elements, perhaps, but with much interacting with people (as well as onions). It was filling in time with a sort of purpose. These people tended to queue for the checkout and a brief chat with the cashier rather than use the automatic payout booths. I was so fascinated that, when my replacement arrived, I stayed on watching.

I remarked on this to a friend who told me that in her country town the cashiers at the local (only) supermarket had been replaced by automatic ones. Not only were residents enraged by the removal of several precious jobs from their community, but it was found that revenues fell markedly as shoppers took their custom to the greengrocer, butcher, hardware store – places where there was still human interaction. If you live alone or on a remote property, passing the time of day with another soul, a human is an important part of your shopping. I shop as much as I can at my local market. The food is fresh, the choice is wonderful, the conversations brief but funny. And I am treated as a *person*. I *matter*.

ACTIVITIES, CLUBS AND THE INTERNET

Tennis, golf, book clubs all provide good, active company for some. I have deep interests in various branches of the arts and low-water gardening, and I find that the members of the clubs I belong to have knowledge I long to absorb and different viewpoints that make me think. They open many fascinating doors of interest in my life. Thank you Tim and Kathy, Bernadette and Relton, Rae, Patricia, Caroline, John, Noeline, Attila and Michelle, Heinz, Wayne, Victor, Andrew, Anton, Caroline, Susie, Robin, Sarah, Chloe, Maria, Olga, Margaret, Jan, Robert, Michel, Bruce, Isobel, Caroline, Louise, Vicki, Amanda, Sue.

The Men's Shed movement[36] worldwide seems to fulfil a great need. Its motto is: 'Men don't talk face to face they talk shoulder to shoulder'. Men's Sheds provide a means of meeting like-minded people, sharing a skill, maybe learning a new one, doing something useful and perhaps even providing an excuse to absent oneself from home! I don't have first-hand experience of these, but I hope they throw in couple of well-deserved beers while they are at it!

Another gem is The Dull Men's Club[37]: pea shooting, photographing roundabouts, sitting on a park bench, apostrophe protection. You name it. Dull? An eight-hour movie starring sheep? The Dull Man of the Year? Reading their website, I began feeling it was one of the more exciting things around. Alas, this is only in the United States and the United Kingdom (so far) but the ideas are inspiring, cheering, and funny. Best of all, you don't even have to be a man to access their website!

FRIENDSHIPS

Love after Love

The time will come
when, with elation,
you will greet yourself arriving
at your own door, in your own mirror
and each will smile at the other's welcome,
and say, sit here. Eat.

---

[36] www.amsa@menshed.net
[37] www.dullmensclub.com

You will love again the stranger who was yourself.
Give wine. Give bread. Give back your heart.
to itself, to the stranger who has loved you
all your life, whom you ignored
for another, who knows you by heart.
Take down the love letters from the bookshelf,
the photographs, the desperate notes,
peel your own image from the mirror.
Sit. Feast on your life.

~Derek Walcott

The Welsh have fifteen words for 'home'. The Norwegians, I am told, have eleven words for snow. There are fifteen words, apparently, that describe the smell of a ripe durian fruit. Our language has very few satisfactory alternatives for 'friend'. My thesaurus lists 23, but most are obsolete.

That is extraordinary, if you think about it, since there are as many kinds and qualities of friendships as there are, evidently, of snow. The word 'friend' lumps together people from many parts of your life: school and cousins, university and work, professional colleagues, people with shared interests, even a dog. Our partner's colleagues, friends, relations. sports. All of these are different types of friends who wield a different power within our lives, and not all of them will stand the test of time. Some friends you can collapse into and they are as soft and enveloping as a snowdrift, others are fairly slippery and you have to take care how you walk; and some melt at the smallest bit of sun or sadness. Many people have lives so busy with career, children, the next marathon, further study, elderly, sick, or small grandchildren needing to be collected early, that 'life' gets forgotten in the swirl. Remember that it is not the number of social contacts you have that is important, but the quality of them.

Our society seems to find it hard to acknowledge with kindness that a life-change has occurred with a bereavement. You can collapse helplessly in a chair and trust that family and friends will rally around to support and help you. And they will – *for a while*. But many bereaved people, and widows especially, feel that few friends visit once the first dramatic flush of mourning is over.

One of the most common experiences, often remarked upon after a big life-change such as divorce or death, is that friends melt away. If friends seem to fade, remember it is not *you* who is lacking. People find it hard to put simple regret, simple sadness into words. Many widows, and divorcees especially, find when de-partnered they are no longer invited by friends who had always welcomed them with gladness in the past. It seemed to take a while before people were comfortable with me in my new status. My children would say: "it sucks!" But it makes me all the gladder when I am smilingly invited to anything, for any reason. I know I am really, truly and warmly welcome, for myself and not as part of a couple.

The Countess Mountbatten of Burma, who was crippled in an IRA bombing that murdered her husband, her son and other Royal family members, said people she knew would avoid her, on occasion crossing to the other side of the road. What she wanted was to talk about the tragedy, she said. What her friends wanted was to avoid doing so. So, it happens to everyone, whoever they may be. That may or may not be of comfort!

'Suttee' is still practised in the more primitive parts of India. The widow is thrown, live, onto the funeral pyre of her husband. This saves the community having to feed a mouth whose provider has gone, it would also save the embarrassment that people in our societies feel with the newly widowed. But in my opinion, experiencing minor embarrassment is infinitely preferable to being unwillingly barbecued!

At a funeral a while ago, six of my husband's friends gathered around me. They had tears in their eyes. How they missed him they said, his dreadful puns, his laughter: their fun lunches were not such fun anymore. They had each written to me when he died, nice letters full of regret, but not one of them had phoned me – not after he died, nor in the years since, to say they were sorry he had gone or to ask how was I getting on. I knew my husband would have been sorry about that. I smiled. I quietly said goodbye and walked away. Far from being sad, I felt as if I had put down a suitcase that carried much of my old life and old memories, and that I walked on lighter of heart as a consequence.

RE-PARTNERING

Men who lose their partners are often overwhelmed with care. 'Casserole brigades' can strike fear into the staunchest male heart I hear, but divorced men and widowers can also suffer overpowering loneliness. Remarriage appears to be more tempting for men than women – plenty of studies have found that men are more likely to remarry, often quickly. (Record for speed, recounted in a recent book is the man who married the lady who directed his first wife's funeral!). People I have known who have had an unhappy marriage often yearn to find the happiness that has eluded them first time around, but women are statistically less likely to remarry than men.

Internet dating is said to be interesting. I have heard hilarious reports of glorious, memorable, enjoyable matching and, (in retrospect) mismatching.

Myself: I ironed a shirt for a son. I was surprised how much I hated doing so. 41 years x 365 days = 14,965 shirts, at least, I had ironed in my married life. This was approximately the 14,966th. I decided I could not ever iron shirts again. Ever.

Would I have wanted to re-partner? Perhaps. But I am too tired to find that tempting. I feel I run faster but get everywhere slower. One thing I know, I could never bear to sit beside another love and slowly, slowly watch him die.

Also, there is a difficulty. Socialising can throw up unexpected problems. I laugh a lot, and it is terrible at jolly gatherings to see a wife looking across a room and mistaking my laughter at a funny joke for flirtation with her husband. I was recently told (smugly, by someone still married) that a widow could be seen by others as a reminder that it (death) can happen to anyone: a walking reminder that life is fragile, and she can also be viewed as a threat.

I think that nothing is more stimulating than a well-chosen table of six or eight thoughtful and intelligent people, but an unexpected hazard of being a widow is inviting a single man to dinner – you can be suspected of having designs on him. An old friend had died a few months before. I was having a congenial bunch of people to dinner, numbers were odd, and I asked her husband to join us. He was clever, interesting and I thought he might like a bit of diversion and a good dinner. The next time I saw his daughter she bounced up to me with a huge grin and said, "Thank you! Dad did enjoy that evening. Oh we had such fun – we all teased him and said, 'Dad oooohhh! You look out!'". I had wanted to do no more than a good turn for a sad old friend, but have I dared repeat the gesture? No, of course not! Moreover, I will think hard before asking a single man ever again, however unhappy, hungry or lonely he looks. How sad.

HAPPINESS

I have often noticed that when someone talks about a difficult time in their life when they had to think themselves out of a difficulty, they often dwell on how much they learned from the bad and the sad experiences. To me, sadness means I survive, that I cared. If I am sad it implies that I lost something that was worth having. Surely that sums up any life worth living. It is possible not to lose your sadness but to make yourself live with it happily. That may not be the best choice of words in this context, but it works for me. Consider what is right in your life and begin from there.

We all know we can sit ourselves down in a chair and, by casting our minds over things that enrage or upset us can work up a case of mild depression in about 15 minutes. You can achieve full-scale misery in half an hour if you concentrate hard enough.

Knowing that, do the opposite. Say: 'Yes, I am upset/enraged/heartbroken' (whichever fits the bill). But then say: 'I am alive, I must live as best I can, while life is mine'. Try again. Say: 'How lucky I have been' and not 'How unfortunate I am'. Hopefully you will find that the load you carry – even if it is the same load – feels lighter.

One in ten people (one in four of the young, some say) are said to be on antidepressants. OK. Helps. Maybe. For a while. But the problem that caused it may not go away. Grief is not an illness or a disorder. Grief may be muted by time, but it cannot be cured only by pills. If you believe it is the *pill* that helped you then you may not make the discovery that you can grow, make yourself stronger, more resilient on your own *without* pills. It seems to me that people who use their inner resources to shape and change themselves attain in the end a confidence that they can control their life and make it into something they can live with. Always speak with a health professional when it comes to taking or stopping prescribed medication.

Older women are said to score the highest in happiness surveys. I find I *know* I am content, mainly because I know what it is like to be unhappy. I am *aware* I am serene because I know what it feels like to be in turmoil. I *feel* confident because I have experienced the fright of not being sure. I feel it is nothing to do with being older or a woman, it is to do with knowing that you have been able to find ways to survive difficulties.

I find it harder to decide exactly what is happiness than I used to. It is a miserable day today, as I write: cold, breezy, rain. I would once have said it is a horrid day. But rain can be scarce where I live. It is a treasured friend of the earth. So I look out of my window and say, "This is what the earth needs – this is good".

It seems to me that it is only if you are able to enjoy small pleasures that you are equipped to also enjoy bigger ones. So, work-out, walk, crossword, coffee in a favourite mug. Learn what works for you. With me, I *have* to look at clouds every day. I even find myself mesmerised by the blue when there are no clouds to watch! If you live alone there will be days where you find the misty grey fingers of despair are plucking at your seams, pulling, fraying the hems of your life. Take note if the small pleasures pall. Take action before you find that those grey fingers have turned into a black fist which has you firmly in its grip. If you fall into a pit of gloom, it is the small, inconsequential pleasures that will form the (wobbly) ladder that helps you climb out and back into an equable life.

I have a tiny vase the size of an egg. It takes one short-stemmed flower. I love flowers but I have come to understand that it is not only the flowers that give me pleasure. As I put out my hand to pick one, even a daisy, I realise that I am affirming to myself that I value the pleasure they will give me, that I value myself enough to give myself that pleasure. *That I matter.*

That was only a small thing. It helped me. I needed the small help as well as the bigger help. You may need a more robust course of action. Find what works for you. You may find that antidepressants and a good therapist are more helpful and perhaps even essential than my small vase and crochet.

Consolation can come from unexpected quarters. One day I saw a wonderful abstract painting in soft greys, lavenders, pinks. I decided I would crochet myself a jacket in the same colours. I had hardly crocheted since my grandmother had taught me at her knee. This turned into a hilarious exercise. Every time I dwelt on an anxiety or sadness I found myself changing either the colour or the stitch. There were frills and stripes, patches and flaps, bobbles and wobbles. The result was a cross between a textile textbook and a gypsy-camp collaboration, but the soft pelt of it growing beneath my fingers brought a certain serenity, a curious peace.

I showed it off, proudly, to my children. A daughter looked at it and said, "Mum, how wonderful." A son, after a thoughtful pause, and possibly more honest, said, "Mum, be careful where you wear that!" The memories woven into its fabric are sad, glad, powerful... and in a strange way, comforting. I think I shall ask to be dressed in it when I die – it will burn nicely.

It is important to learn to squeeze pleasure from everything that can give pleasure. I have decided that happiness mostly comes in small, glorious flashes rather than broad, shapeless sweeps. I have many friends who dye their hair. That is of small interest you might think. But with me it is a very deliberate choice not to do so. My hair is nearly white, and I like it that way. To me it is an affirmation that I have accepted my age and stage, that I have achieved a certain peace with myself and the world.

But it is more. I feel I have earned every single one of those white hairs, from things that were hard but which I thought I could manage or endure, but also things that I never knew I was strong enough to bear. My grandchildren look at me and understand. I am different – I *look* different. My children (I hope) look on me and *know* that I *know*. This is my right path. It is strange to me that the power of a proclaimed appearance – white hair – can throw such a blanket of comfort around my life. Besides, when my hair is entirely white, I have an awful suspicion that I will do what I have always wanted to do – to have little pink stripes put in all over. Silly? Yes. Fun? Sure.

Life rushes past at headlong speed. The sand roars ever louder through the hourglass. You can either reach out and grab it as it goes by, or you can sit in a chair and watch it go past. You can seize and chew the goodness out of it (remembering to spit out the pips!), or sit and chew the cud. What a choice. Neither of these is right or wrong, but only one of them will be right for you at any one particular moment in time. I decided on the former – to enjoy every moment of life while I can but if there comes a time when the latter is preferable, then I shall change and become a watcher. It may not actually be this simple. But you have to begin somewhere, and this helped me.

Comfort does come. Several years on I saw some earrings. I fell in love with them. They were aqua, soft coloured, beautiful. I heard my husband's voice over my shoulder, clear as a bell: 'The red ones are nice, try the red.' He had always liked colour. 'Or the yellow, what about the yellow.' I nearly laughed aloud – perhaps I did. After a bit of thought, I bought the aqua. The colour looked soft, good against my grey hair. Perhaps I was becoming softer of mood, less in need of vivid colour too. But I was strangely cheered. My husband might have left this world, but he had in no way left my life.

CHAPTER EIGHT

Fantastic facts, strange statistics, different traditions, and new ways of disposing of the dead and memorialising

There is no advice in this chapter, just fascinating facts, so... keep reading.

METHODS OF DISPOSING OF THE DEAD

The increasing numbers of dead are a growing world problem.

The dead can impact upon the living in unexpected ways. In France, beginning in 1786, six million bodies (some over 1,000 years old) were moved from old cemeteries when the height of accumulated burials had caused some cemetery walls to collapse. Bodies were put on large, black covered carts and moved under cover of darkness, and arranged neatly in the old stone and gypsum quarries which surrounded Paris. There are over 300 kilometres of catacombs[38] –

---
38   www.thecorpseproject.net

avenues of skulls and bones, some arranged in extraordinary patterns – under the streets of Paris. You can visit these catacombs, but choose a priority tour – it is very popular, and the queues can be long. The catacombs are not scary, however, be careful not to be left behind your group. That *is* scary. Interestingly, because re-buried skeletons are loose and fragmentary it can be difficult to construct strong foundations for houses in these areas, which is the reason why many parts of Paris do not have tall buildings.

The City of London has many small public gardens. Some are just a bench and a few roses. My mother-in-law was on the committee that looked after these. She told me that they were the site of old plague pits. In plague times a cart would drive round the at night. The cry would go out: "Bring out your dead!" It is forbidden to disturb or build on these, whether out of respect for the dead or fear that the contagion could escape, I do not know.

It has been suggested that double land-use should be bought in, so that cows can graze on land where bodies have been buried, for instance. Though bodies only provide accessible nutrients if they are buried in fairly shallow graves. Graveyards have been used for solar panels in Barcelona, Spain or turned into playgrounds in Germany – a secondary advantage being that this protects the land from developers.

Our society is on the brink of a demographic catastrophe. Life expectancy has increased by ten years across the globe in the past thirty-five years, and the number of people aged 65 and over has more than tripled in 50 years. The country with the lowest life expectancy is Chad (north-central Africa) at 49.81 years, and the highest is Monaco at 89.52 years, (Japan is second at 83.75). In Australia it is 82.8 years. But *"healthspan"* – the number of years lived in relatively good health – has not increased as much as *lifespan*, meaning we live longer, but we often spend many years with challenging health problems. How much has changed in recent times. Michel de Montaigne who died in 1592 wrote that death in old age was a "rare, singular and extraordinary" occurrence. Nowadays it is the norm.

It has been calculated that life expectancy in Roman times was 28 years. Some people would attain a great age, but the infant mortality rate was very high. Two Viking cemeteries were recently analysed – the average age of death in one was 20s the other 30s. It is thought that death in combat probably accounted to 15% of deaths in such early communities, but the main cause of death is thought to be epidemics and malnutrition. Imagine the grief that these communities lived with. It is said that amongst sailors and seamen there were 100 deaths from scurvy for every one of them killed in combat.

Nowadays we are insulated from death. We are more likely to die in a hospital, away from home. We are more likely to die because we are old than in an epidemic (COVID notwithstanding). We are more likely to die from over-eating than famine. In 2016 worldwide deaths related to obesity numbered 3 million, terrorists killed 25,600 people yet we seem to be more frightened of a terrorist than we are of our waistlines! Opioids are driving down life expectancy in the US – drug overdoses killed 63,600 people in the US in 2016. If you are young, you are more likely to die from an overdose than anything else.

Most of us are cured of ailments which in years past would have carried us off. We are living longer but we may find ourselves living longer with age-related hearing, sight impairment, osteoarthritis, cancers and dementia. We may have been diagnosed with chronic life-sentences such as diabetes, obesity, disability caused by recreational drug use and smoking. We may be permanently on heart/blood/HIV drugs which sometimes have terrible side effects. We are told we can 'fight' cancer. Does that mean if we die we 'lose the battle' and have not fought hard enough? We have been trained to expect that sophisticated medical intervention will result in a very high rate of successful outcomes; if the patient dies then the doctor, surely, has failed.

But the day we are born we arrive with an expiry date etched into our futures. This can change due to accident, increased medical knowledge, carelessness. Over the last decades death has largely been professionalised, put into hospitals and removed from homes. But as a health worker put it nicely: "Death is not a medical event, it is a social event with medical input." We accept death, splattering and screaming its' way bloodily across TV/movie screens, but in real life, pale, final and loved we seem not to be able to face it at all. We do not talk about it – it is the new 'no-no'. We now fear death where previous generations accepted that it was part of a natural cycle.

Some interesting statistics: Dr Katherine Sleemen of King's College London has been quoted as saying that in the United Kingdom about one fifth of deaths are sudden, such as accidents. A further fifth follows a swift decline, as with many cancer patients, who stay fairly active until the last few weeks. Three-fifths come after (on average) eight to ten years of relapse and recovery that involves slow progressive deterioration of function. Falls are one of the greatest dangers – 40% of elderly people who fall end up in nursing homes and 20% are never able to walk again. If there is anyone in your life to whom this may apply, check for hazards such as rugs which can be tripped on.

China and Japan after many years of low birth-rates have looming, agonising problems with their ageing populations. More adult nappies are sold in Japan than baby ones. 15,000 elderly Japanese are said to be driven far from home each year and abandoned; some municipalities there are now insisting that the elderly have barcodes sewn onto their clothes, so if found wandering they can be returned to their families.

It is said that an eighth of Americans with terminal cancer receive chemotherapy in their final fortnight, even though it is of no benefit at such a late stage. Nearly a third of elderly Americans undergo surgery during their final year, and 8% do so in their last week. Interestingly, worldwide you are more likely to be murdered on a Sunday (unless you are in prison when it is Mondays that should make you nervous), die in a car crash on a Saturday, commit suicide on a Monday, be born on a Tuesday. It is remarkable, apparently, how many people die on their birthdays (perhaps after more alcohol than usual at a jolly celebration?).[39]

Attitudes to suicide have varied throughout history and also in

---

[39] US Center for Disease Control and Prevention Report: Average number of deaths from motor vehicle injuries, suicide and homicide.

various religions. Japan has a tradition of honourable suicides; for instance, over 2,500 Kamikaze pilots died during the course of World War II, which seems to me to be State-sanctioned suicide. The Jewish tradition has laws which forbid suicide, the Roman Catholic church also considers it a mortal sin. In the Muslim world death in the course of jihad is considered to be martyrdom, not suicide. Hindus will accept suicide by fasting – because it is a considered action and is not acting on impulse. The Romans considered it a noble act in certain circumstances. Suicide is high in many indigenous communities world-wide especially in young males. This is thought to be largely due to the changing traditions in such societies where the old certainties and support systems, are in a state of flux.

In Australia in 2015 there were more than 3,000 suicides, more than double the number of deaths on the roads. It is the leading cause of death for people between 15 and 44. In the US there are over 30,000 suicides each year, in the United Kingdom 6,000. (Per 100,000: United States 11.8; United Kingdom 7.00; Australia10.8.) It is said there are roughly 25 non-fatal suicide attempts per every successful one. Each suicide is said to leave on average six deep mourners, and there is a particularly high rate of deep, complicated, long-term grief connected to deaths by suicide. Suicide support groups, and even internet support groups are said to be very helpful.

BODY FARMS

There are eight body farms in the United States, none in Europe. At the Centre for Forensic Science at the University of Technology in Sydney, Professor Shari Forbes opened the first one in Australia in 2015 and has already been inundated with offers (at the time of writing over 850 in prospect). Body farms were instituted to study the process of human decomposition. Bodies decompose at very different rates according to the environment, the depth of burial etc. A *necro biome* develops around decaying organic matter. Affected by such things as humidity, soil microbes, shallow/deep burial, insects, carnivores, scavengers etc., which can vary greatly from place to place. In dry Australian conditions bodies often swiftly mummify and are then difficult to date.

In the past, research was done on pigs, but it has been found that pigs decompose in a very different way to humans. Research is necessary to help coroners and police investigate the possible date of deaths, and also to help police to train police dogs (cadaver dogs) to find corpses, often many years old from war crimes, bombings, earthquakes, floods and murders. I understand that provision has to be made to prevent wild animals and raptors disturbing the corpses in a body farm. Police are experimenting using drones equipped with lidar scanning technology. Signals are sent, which, even thorough dense forest cover, can discover places where the soil has been disturbed. This may prove to be a valuable tool to uncover mass graves in conflict areas.

CRYOGENICS

Cryogenics anyone? They freeze you (-196 degrees in nitrogen). The hope is that when you are revived many years hence a cure will have been found for whatever ailed you when you died, but you will be the same age, thawed, as when you died. As far as I can see your partner will be a winkled prune, while you may still look young and lithe when (if) you emerge. A strange experience for both of you! You may find you are the same age as your youngest great-grandchild. Meanwhile, your estate, (you need to be moneyed to even contemplate the costs) would not have helped their parents afford their education. I hope they would welcome you back.

In Australia, Southern Cryonics is hoping to build a storage facility at Holbrook, in southern NSW. I have heard it has 27 founding members at $50,000 per person, but that the cost will leap to $150,000 once the facility is established.

Another approach to lengthening life is that of the futurist Ray Kurzweil who, approaching 70, is determined to extend his lifespan. He takes 150 pills and vitamins a day. "You can stay young," he says, "until we have even more knowledge to become even younger." If I ate 150 pills a day, I think I would have no room for food. His autopsy will be interesting.

I cannot help feeling that those contemplating avenues of aggressive life-lengthening might be more in need of spiritual guidance than a deep freeze or pills!

INFINITY BURIAL SUIT

Perhaps there will be more alternatives available in the future. I quote from *The Art Newspaper* No 315 September 2019: "The Korean-born, California-based artist Jae Rhim Lee's burial suit offers an eco-friendly funeral option. The biodegradable suit is embedded with mycelium spores that spawn mushrooms and evokes Tibetan-style burials, where the dead return to the earth through natural decomposition ... traditional Western burial and cremation methods pollute the environment ... this fungus-powered suit aids decomposition and releases nutrients to the surrounding plants and soil. Lee created the suit as part of her graduate programme at the Massachusetts Institute of Technology." The suit and shroud are sold for US$1,500.[40]

In the United States, Olson Kundig Architecture has designed an after-death facility where corpses will be turned into compost. In Florida, funeral directors are developing a new technology – alkaline hydrolysis or "liquid cremation" – dissolving the body until nothing but a fairly harmless bio-fluid is left which can then be flushed away. In Seattle, a system has been developed: 'Recompose' where bodies are placed in modular vessels with woodchips and turned into nutrient-rich soil. And a Swedish researcher is working on a scheme to freeze-dry bodies prior to chipping and composting them so they can be used as garden fertiliser. The euthanasia advocate Philip Nitschke has created a very smart-looking 3D printed suicide machine (a photograph shows a bright blue pod with a glass top) and, by pressing a button on the inside of the pod, liquid nitrogen is released which makes the user feel 'slightly' tipsy before falling unconscious then dying. I do wonder how they found out about the 'sightly tipsy'. The pod can then be used as a coffin if desired.

It is interesting to think of the people I have met who have made it plain that they felt that the world deserves, and would benefit, from having them for longer. I have to tell you that I like them less, and

---

40 www.coeio.com

feel they are of less value to humanity than others I have met who, triumphant achievers, still try to get the last bits done, the last sip out of the cup of life before they have to bow, gracefully, to the Grim Reaper and prepare themselves to hand over to another generation as keen and avid for life as they have been.

My father, who at 103 was driving, shopping and cooking for himself, broke his shoulder aged 104. Still sharp, we had to cancel a BBC team due to interview him the week he was hospitalised. He hated being dependent on others. He said that he felt that his page in history had been turned and he looked forward to death. His sharpness of mind was of no comfort to him now. He took the only course that our kind, caring society leaves open to someone in his position, and one that a doctor friend says is remarkably common. He stopped eating.

Our present approach to life – that we are entitled to live until we stop breathing – has not been shared by other societies. Although Neolithic bones have been found with signs of such advanced arthritis that the individual would have been dependent on the care of their community, in times of famine or siege it would have been essential for a tribe to save only those needed for their long-term survival: the young, the wise, the strong warriors and the young women. I once saw the annual migration of the Qashqai tribe in Iran in the early '70s. It was a most beautiful sight. A whole plain was dotted with people walking singly, some in pairs, the occasional threesome. Not one of the horses was being ridden, they were loaded with bedding. Clothing? Cooking pots? Anyone who could not walk was left behind, I was told, as it would threaten the survival chances of the whole group. The Spartans would expose newly born babies on a hill overnight, so that only those that were fit would survive. The moment an Eskimo woman's eldest daughter bore a child she would be taken out and put behind a nice, soft snowdrift. There is no snow where I live. Thank goodness.

Different traditions for funerals

Nowadays we are all likely to have a broad friendship/family base and it can be helpful to understand something about the variety of customs surrounding death in order not to make embarrassing mistakes.

Burial customs often have their roots deep in the past. The Roman Catholic church believes that the body needs to be whole in order to rise on the day of Resurrection, which meant that cremation was forbidden. This was relaxed in 1963, and cremation is now permitted although Catholics should note that The Vatican insists that ashes are interred rather than scattered. It is interesting to remember that the real point of the old punishment of hanging (painful), drawing (agonising) and quartering (deadly) was that the body, quartered and scattered, would not be able to be resurrected on Judgement Day, was not just death in this world – it was death for ever after.

There were tears in the eyes of an elderly man as he told me of the burial of his godfather, a Duke of Argyll. It had been a conventional church service but afterwards the mourners stood on the shore as the coffin was rowed away to the island where the Dukes were traditionally interred. Echoes of a Viking sea-burial? Or crossing the ancient River Styx? The boat was quickly swallowed up in the heavy, swirling mist but the sound of the bagpipe and the oars could be heard for a long time after, fading slowly, slowly. The symbolism was powerful, strong.

It is interesting to remember that the gold earring favoured by mariners (and pirates) was intended, if you were lost or buried at sea, to be the payment to Charon so that he would row your body across the River Styx (or Lethe, or Acheron) to the land of the dead on the other side.

ABORIGINAL

Rites and traditions differ greatly from group to group. The 'Sorry Business' and the ceremonies can spread over several days. Generally, Australian aboriginals find it immensely offensive if the name of the departed is uttered. On radio and television, a warning is always given if the name of a recently departed member of the aboriginal community is about to be mentioned so that anyone likely to be offended can turn off the program. It is advisable to take care how you word references and condolences in such communities. I would love to know how long this prohibition lasts – if forever, it would mean that stories about ancient heroes, innovators, disasters could not be related round a campfire, and learnt from and relished.

In some places (such as the Kimberley, Northern Australia) bones are placed on an elevated platform, and once clean and dry are painted with red ochre. This custom seems to have lasted the 42,000 years (dated by thermoluminescence) since the time of Lake Mungo burials. It is interesting that the earliest burials found in Europe also have bones painted with red ochre.

JEWISH

In the Jewish tradition the dead must not be left alone and are buried, ideally, within 24 hours. Someone from Chevra Kadisha arrives immediately to sit with the dead, as should at least one male relative. Burial is in a simple coffin, with the body wrapped in a shroud. I have only once been to a Jewish funeral, a great friend. It was a simple occasion plainly meant for the family only. You do not dress up for a Jewish funeral, indeed a pair of scissors may be handed round to cut off men's ties or cut clothing – an ancient tradition: in the Bible the custom was 'to *rend*' (or tear) your clothing. Check that your presence will be welcome if you want to attend a Jewish funeral – it may be a better choice to call on the family during Shiva.

Jewish families sit 'minyan' on the night of the funeral. Then most Jewish families continue sitting Shiva (shiva = seven) – a week of mourning in which they sit, with bathing, make-up and perfume forbidden, mirrors covered, and doing nothing other than thinking of and mourning the departed. The community will bring food and the family receives visits of condolence. Do not send flowers; symbolic of celebration, they are considered inappropriate. A Jewish friend laughed as he said what with all the coming and going, the food being brought/shared round and the chatting as people inevitably got bored just sitting, Shiva is often a most enjoyable time. At the end of a week the bereaved get up and are expected to continue life as normal.

There is a lovely custom in this community. Sometimes it is hard to know what to say to the newly bereaved, and their tradition is simply to hold the person's arms and say simply, "I wish you long life."

MUSLIM

Death is viewed as the start of real life – his or her eternal life. A dying Muslim may want to die facing Mecca and will be buried facing Mecca. The body is washed according to gender, by family members or friends and then wrapped in several shrouds. Muslims are buried swathed in a shroud but without a coffin. Muslims, like Jews, are buried within 24 hours and males, only, accompany the body to burial. Women do not attend funerals. Funeral companies will provide shrouds.

HINDU, SIKH, TAMIL

Hindus believe in reincarnation and think their current situation (station) is due to their behaviour in previous lives, and that the state of a person's mind as they are dying is vital in determining the form of their next reincarnation. They are very caste-conscious, and complicated rituals are used to maintain their 'social' order. Both Hindus and Sikhs cremate their dead. Hindu traditions require that a family remains viewing the conflagration until it is complete. Some crematoriums have glass-lined viewing rooms so that such a family can watch. A bowl is put on top of the coffin, oil is poured into it so that it overflows, and it is then lighted to initiate the burning. The ashes are traditionally cast into running water. It may be useful to know that many Tamils are now Christian.

MĀORI

Alan Preston, of Auckland, has described to me the very different traditions that surround a Māori death: the Tangi can last at least three days. The tupapaku, or body, usually stays at home and then travels to the Marae of the Whanau, family or Hapu, sub-tribe, and people arrive to stay and are welcomed and many songs and speeches happen. The person is then buried in the family urupa, cemetery. Sometime after death there is the Kawemate: the Whanau will go from marae to marae with a group carrying images of the dead person for the people to pay tribute who were not able to attend the Tangi.

NEW GUINEA

Some customs can have unexpected impacts. The For tribe in New Guinea suffered from a disease called The Laughing Sickness. It was discovered in the 1950s that this was the result of funerary practices which involved eating the brains of the newly dead. There are a great number of different tribes all of which have different customs. But the dead are often exposed on high platforms to decay and on the whole are considered to be part of life – the continuum.

AFRICA

Again this vast continent has a huge number of tribes who follow different customs. Many of these do not recognise sickness or age as a reason for death, and in many areas death is supposed to be caused by the malign wishes of enemies etc and revenge is often sought. It may be of interest that in the recent epidemic of Ebola in West Africa the tradition of drinking the water in which the corpse was washed, as well as the handling of it, was thought to have played a large part in spreading the disease.

I saw an exhibition of Ghanaian coffins in Paris... Utterly joyous. The coffins were huge: sports cars, animals. It is believed that the spirit of the dead loved one continues living and deserves joy.

BUDDHIST

It is customary to wear white at Buddhist funerals. Everyone attending is given a coin, a sweet (lolly) and a red ribbon to tie to a tree.

CHINESE

At Chinese funerals, the family will burn joss paper (spirit paper) to ensure their loved one has a safe journey to the netherworld. Attendance at the wake, usually in a restaurant, is by previous invitation only.

IRISH, WELSH, SCOTTISH, MACEDONIAN

If Irish, family members invite individuals they want to attend the wake. The Welsh traditionally do not leave the deceased's home empty during the funeral. In living memory on the Scottish Isles women stayed inside with the coffin mourning loudly. The men stood outside fortifying themselves until 'The Carry': the coffin often had to be carried some distance. Being heavy, it is put down at every telegraph pole, and after a sip the bearers swap places and the 'Carry' resumes. It has been known for a group to arrive at the church and having to be sent back by an irate vicar to fetch the coffin – forgotten along the way! There are 31 Mort Houses, small round windowless stone houses, in Scotland where bodies could be stored if there needed to be a delay in burying them – if the ground was frozen for instance. Macedonians bury the dead after three or so days of mourning and then sit around the grave, hand round baked fish and home-distilled liquor, which it is obligatory to sip. Some ethnic groups, following a tradition that goes back beyond the Romans, remove the bone remnants from the cremation furnace themselves and place them, whole, in an ossuary (traditionally a carved stone or wood box).

OSSUARIES

In countries around the Mediterranean, where the soil is often shallow and rocky, bodies were traditionally interred for three years and the bones were then dug up and cleaned, rinsed with wine, perfumed and with much ceremony and lamentation placed in ossuaries or above ground vaults. In Europe, charnel chapels were used to store old bones, the skulls in one pile, long bones in another. Sometimes they are arranged in intricate, almost beautiful patterns. There is, unbelievably, a name for putting many bones together – *necro-sociability* – companionship in death. When my mother was buried in a small, ancient church I asked the gravedigger if he ever disturbed old bones when he dug. He said sometimes he would disturb the remains of three old corpses when he dug a new grave.

SEVENTH DAY ADVENTIST

Women are often buried in their wedding dresses – as a bride of Christ. Mourning is not allowed – death is considered a joyous event because that person has gone to be with their beloved maker.

WHAT TO DO WITH THE ASHES?

Cemeteries have niches for urns called Columbary Walls but enquire the time limit of these – you often have to renew the space every 25 years. Every cemetery has a place, sometimes wall-niches where memorial plaques can be displayed if there is not an actual grave.

Cremated remains have a very high mineral content. Incineration releases a large amount of mercury (teeth fillings) and arsenic, which is a matter of concern to some health authorities. No waste product, and this includes cremated remains, should be scattered in a water-catchment area. If you wish to scatter cremated remains in a public place, you should get permission to do so from a local port, shire authority, or the like. It is estimated that 70% of ashes are scattered somewhere meaningful, though some people prefer their mantelpiece.

Ben Nevis (a mountain in the United Kingdom) is a popular place to scatter ashes, but they are wreaking havoc with mosses and alpine plants which cannot stand the high levels of calcium and phosphate in human ashes. Many botanic gardens have had to take measures to prevent remains from being scattered there. Professor Tim Entwisle of the Royal Botanic Gardens in Melbourne told me that the gardens had found that the high mineral content of ashes sprinkled there (without permission) was killing some of their oldest and most valued trees. If scattered near shrubs the cremated remains should be mixed with other soil to balance out their high levels of salts and other minerals.

If you wish to bury ashes at sea, ask permission from the port authority – you will be required to take them at least three nautical miles out to sea. It is possible to buy very pretty, biodegradable urns so the ashes can float away. Disney Land has had to take steps to stop people scattering ashes – The Haunted Mansion, is a favourite place, apparently. People do silly things: in the interval of a concert at Covent Garden someone tipped the ashes of his friend, a passionate music lover, into the orchestra pit. The concert had to be abandoned so the ashes (a possible health hazard) could be vacuumed.

It has been suggested that when you scatter ashes you should choose a windy day so that they are distributed over a large area. If so, study the direction of the wind. Friends of a famous poet once scattered his ashes in a solemn ceremony over a cliff. They did not check the wind and found their eyes and their mouth full of *him!*

Never scatter dear Grandpa's ashes on his favourite sports oval (which is often done secretly). Cremated remains are neither benign nor soft. They are sharp and abrasive, and players have been known to have sustained horrific grazes from skidding on unsuspected ashes. Remember, also, that the grass in such places is often rolled up and renewed. Grandpa could exit on a dump truck ☹.

CINERARIUM?

Our church has a small memorial garden where ashes can be interred with a simple dignified ceremony. It is good to know the dead are near us when we are there. But perhaps contemporary cities need huge *cinerariums*.

Imagine an approachable, non-threatening, beautiful, non-denominational building. A pyramidal tower, perhaps, carved with flocks of birds, with various wheel-chair accessible apertures at the top with an area where families can gather to drop in the urn with its ashes with due solemnity for permanent storage? Perhaps for a small fee? And gathering-friendly, with a small playground, or cafe. When ashes are deposited there could be provision to add the names of the dead and a photo to a well-kept data base. Even small biographies that could be called up by historians or future generations or those interested to see a photo of their great-great...? Certainly, a new community-friendly answer needs to be found.

MEMORIALISING

When the funeral is over, deep breaths have been taken, and a little energy is beginning to seep back into veins and brains, the thoughts of a family may turn to making a memorial.

Humankind seems to have an innate need to mark some of the steps in life in a meaningful way. There is often a desire for an acknowledgement, a ritual acceptance for all to share at this special moment, which does not need to have a religious basis.

Since the beginning of time there have been varying ideas and traditions around death and memorialisation – from 'my pyramid must be bigger than his' to the Greek philosopher Demosthenes, who asked for his body to be thrown over the city walls to be scavenged by dogs (that is not now legal, but I suppose you could still get planning permission for a pyramid).

TOMBSTONES

These can provide a fascinating study. Cemeteries sold plots, the most expensive being those which were easy to see from a path. This provided a community with a socially graded hierarchy of death. Tombstones often had family, descriptive, or poetic inscriptions – equivalent to memorialising graffiti! Daisy Bates (one of her husbands was Breaker Morant) after a lifetime of caring for Aborigines in South Australia had just one word on her tombstone – The Aboriginal word KABBARLI: 'Mother'. A broken pillar above a grave indicted a male who had died without issue. When cemeteries were small and local, they were often a place to stroll after church, to greet friends. They were part of the fabric of their community.

It is possible to buy a 'tree burial' on the internet. You are told to place the ashes along with the tree-tube in the ground or ornamental pot. The tree is supposed to flourish on the nutrients found in the ashes. But what happens when you need to re-pot? This would be less expensive than having ashes shot into space, though, which can be done. Even fireworks: *Heavens Above Fireworks* fill fireworks with ashes so that the deceased can be sent off with a bang.[41]

Releasing white doves is a 'greener' alternative to both, as they return to their roost and can be used again.

An industry has grown up around death. Funeral directors offer many ways of turning your loved one into a memento. You can buy sweet little silver urns for the ashes. You can buy lockets with a compartment at the back. A woman put her husband's ashes under the bed and the dog's ashes in a locket round her neck ("the husband would have roared with laughter,", said Mr Davies, the undertaker, who had known him). Another widow puts her husband's ashes in her bed each night. You can buy a teddy bear kit, especially in the case of babies or the stillborn, that is filled with ashes that you can carry around with you and cuddle. You can commission 'memory stones' or paperweights with a swirl of the ashes incorporated.

The funeral directors InvoCare have a new service: a 'digital legacy platform' which enables people to create memorials online for a loved one or even for themselves. These will not be shared until years later, after the death of the person concerned. It strikes me that this could be kind and interesting but, in the wrong hands it could be a vehicle for revenge, untruths and unpleasantness.

You can, also, at great expense, have the ashes turned into diamonds. The ones I saw were about the size of a large pea, and you can choose the colour. I saw lustrous sapphire and a rich, rich red, the colour of blood. Both were flawless. I suppressed a smile. Would such a stone made from my ashes not be permitted to have a few small flaws? These stones take about a year to achieve.

As I write, a family in Portugal is in litigation because their much-loved patriarch had been made into a very small diamond, but only one of his daughters was able to wear him! A company in America makes a ceramic glaze from human ashes – you can sip your coffee from a cup covered with granny's ashes, or else have them incorporated into a vinyl record. And, (America again), Vedstone makes videos showing pictures of the dead person set to music and

---

41   www.heavensabovefireworks.com

placed in a solar-powered screen on a headstone. This is banned in England. One heavily tattooed man had his mother's ashes turned to ink (carbon, after all) and had himself tattooed with it so that she would never leave him.

Geoff Ostling has arranged for his heavily (and beautifully) tattooed skin to go to the National Gallery of Australia after he dies. It takes all kinds – and the diversity in our communities means that there are many options for us to remember those we love.

I have a special place in my heart for such remembrances, and personally I think that is the best solution of all.

CHAPTER NINE

Other people's stories

We all have stories about life and death, but we do not often talk about them. If this book is ever chosen by a book group, I am sure it will give rise to such a flood of memories that everyone will discuss their own stories rather than the book itself!

We all take an interest in other people's disasters and how they did or did not cope. There can be a grim pleasure in finding your situation is far, far more dreadful than someone else's, but sometimes someone else's catastrophe can make one's own disaster seem all the lighter. Or it can point clearly to a thoughtful path it would be good to take.

One day a friend told me her troubles – the child whose uncontrollable addiction had cast a shadow on their past, their future, their career, their finances, their life – as well as over hers. She was helpless, she said, she had done everything she could think of but nothing was of use. Her life was an ongoing, rolling disaster with no apparent solution that either of us could think of. We did not talk about me or my difficulties. I had joined her that day feeling like a tragedy queen, but as she talked, I began to understand that my problem was simple. Mine had a beginning (a pale, flat body lying still) and a clearly desired end – that I could live with the sadness and hopefully enjoy life again.

My problems had a *possible* end. Hers did not. I realised that I had not been the unhappiest person around the table that day. I gave her an extra big hug as we parted.

We all find different mechanisms to help us tackle life. What works for one person does not work for another. I have a dear friend whose way of declaring war upon the world and affirming her love of being alive is to rev her motorised sit-on seat as fast as it will possibly go (downhill that is quite fast) and zoom! She can't stop laughing as she tells me. I have heard laws are about to be introduced where she lives to control this. My friend thinks she does it when it is safe. I think she does it when she needs to. It would be such a pity if well-meaning laws stopped such fun!

Feelings of utter helplessness can engulf some people. I sat with a friend of many years. I could feel her hands shaking as they held mine: "What shall I do? He always told me what to do. How will I know what to do now?" This, a glorious woman who had turned down a United Kingdom peerage for the work she did in the United Nations (a high-caste Brahmin: "It's against my religion to benefit from the good works I have done."). I did not know what to say. She was completely and utterly lost. She had had a lifetime of exceptional achievement, exceptional companionship but had no preparation for the agony of knowing how to decide on her own, the essential – what to do next.

After a glorious, if challenging evening with a French friend, I commented that the whole company was, in some way, single. *"Oui,"* she said, *"in Paris many of us are célibataire* (celibate/single)." She had had a husband, I knew, and a beloved love, a celebrated jazz drummer who had died, much mourned. She paused, looked into the distance, into the past perhaps, and then smiled. She was happy. She had had love. She had been loved. Hers was a good world.

It is interesting that some people cannot see how they can be seen by others: a man tells everyone how wonderful his wife was and how much he misses her. But he laughs ruefully as he recounts how, when she died (a slow, long cancer), he had to get the neighbour in to show him how to use the toaster.

Grieving is needed. I bumped into a good old friend, an antique dealer whose wife had recently died. He looked miserable. He and his wife had always seemed to have their heads together examining, discussing their latest find, their newest and most exciting treasure. They acted as one. I asked how he was. Glancing over his shoulder to see that we were not overheard he said, "In my chapel (a small, unusual sect) we do not mourn. We clap our hands and say joyously 'She's gone to Jesus!', but... I miss her." I stood by him as, shoulders slumped, he grieved, as he needed to grieve, for his beloved, irreplaceable wife and best friend.

There is a saying: Death is the hardest gift we can give to someone we love. The telephone went. *Are you at home? Can I come?* A friend walked in, ashen. "My son has just died." We had all danced at his 21st when he, brilliant and fun-loving, had danced the night away wearing a hat – no hair.

The words came out in a torrent. They had not been able to watch him fading in hospital and had asked to bring him home. They had set up home nursing with a morphine machine. The family had been told how to use it. The nurses told them how to give exactly the right dose for the pain: turn it to this mark they said. But do not do this, do not turn this past this mark, it would be too much, it would be fatal. I did not ask, and she did not say. They loved their son more than anything in this world and he died at home among them, peacefully, loved to the last.

Another friend whose husband died after a long illness when she was in her early 40s found life especially hard. Told he had a terminal illness she realised (as I also should have) that in retrospect they should have known he was ill long before he was diagnosed with the terminal nightmare. They had put his tiredness down to middle age, perhaps depression. When he died, she felt that she had lost half her identity, the sense of who she was, she said. She had been a wife and mother – now she felt she was only a mother. Their shared project, she called it, their children who were young and distressed, were now hers, alone. Her daughter aged 11 had not accepted that the death of her father was a real prospect. The 13-year-old son read an article in a newspaper which dealt with various cancers, co-incidentally including his father's – 5% chance of recovery, it said.

He understood and quietly watched and learnt. He is now training to be a doctor. Two older half-brothers could not cope, did not visit, could not face the inevitable. She grieves still for everything her husband misses out on, every milestone reminds her of the gap by her side. A widely admired academic, vibrantly interesting, she needed to keep her career alive, or it would die. She would have loved to have found another companion, but the men she knew went for younger women. Worst of all, she found, was that on hearing she was single the assumption was, that, at her young age she was divorced. Some sadnesses are harder to bear than others. I hope she has many good friends who will listen and understand, and that one day she will be glad of what she had rather than sad at what she has lost. That was the approach I found helpful, but only after a long, long marriage and many, many more years. My attitude is inappropriate for her situation.

I love furniture. The wood, the design, the sheer companionship that a good desk, chair, table has given through someone's life. I was asked to visit a lady with an eclectic collection of chairs ("She needs cheering up." my friend said). There was a treasure house of glorious op shop finds, museum pieces, shabby, fascinating, loved. We had a lovely time ooing and aahing. There was a certain bleakness about the owner. In her early 40s, and after a passionate seven-year relationship that was just about to end in happiness and babies, she had picked up a newspaper to see her beloved announcing his engagement to the young, bosomy media personality beaming on his arm. She had not even been married, but I think she was the saddest widow I have ever met.

Partnerships come in different shapes and sizes. It may be that in those partnerships not acknowledged publicly by society, bereavement can perhaps be even more painful than for a publicly accepted 'widow' or 'widower'. A man called Stan has negotiated the somewhat turbulent terrain of his life with glorious grace and good humour. He had married his best friend at school but, though still friends with her and their children, had finally accepted that his life and his nature did not lie in that direction. He met Leo, his life-time partner. Though both had professional careers they decided to go busking. I can imagine that they were a compelling double act. He remembers with joy some of their keenest supporters – one, a woman, wore mini-skirts and no knickers, but loved doing the can-can to their music. Her presence always guaranteed a cheering crowd who egged her on unmercifully. Department stores, restaurants, embassies asked them to play. One day his partner had trouble placing his fingers on the violin strings. This turned out to be the start of a long battle with Parkinson's, nursed the entire way, lovingly, by Stan. His whole world crumbled; he still dissolves into a sad reverie at the thought of his lost partner.

A homosexual friend, when asked his opinion on same-sex marriage said, "Why would we want to be part of an institution that you heterosexuals have so discredited?" So I suppose there is room for all kinds of opinions on the subject. But I think we are all glad that there is now a system in place that enables public recognition of loving, long-term partnerships.

Christmas puts life in perspective for me. It is always a salutary reminder that none of us has it forever. The Christmas table seems to me like a train going through my life. Many dear people have got off at earlier stations. Some, who left a long time ago, I know only by repute. Others, aging, still journey with me. Small, new, keen faces join us from time to time and get bigger each year. Suddenly they bring partners, add babies.

One day I will alight at my due platform in eternity and stand on the platform, smiling, and no doubt with tears pricking, wave them all goodbye as they continue their journey through this strange, frightening, exhilarating and unendingly fascinating world. I don't think I believe in an afterlife, but I hope I will live on in the memories of those who knew me for a little while before I, too, am swallowed up into the great wide mist of forgetting. I think we die twice: once when our bodies stop, and secondly when we are forgotten. By this measure, Alexander, Jesus, Mohammed, Napoleon and Churchill still live on.

Shock

Alas, I needed to add this:

My daughter phoned a friend, a nurse. "You don't sound too good," said the friend.

"No,", said my daughter. "Call an ambulance."

The friend called the ambulance and then rang me. I jumped straight in the car. When I reached her house, Steven Gelagotis and Emily Woods from the ambulance team were standing on the pavement outside. "She raised the blind and looked out at us," they said. "But she is not opening the door."

They went in and when they came out, said to me, "She has passed."

Passed? *Passed?* What were they saying? There was a back door. Had she passed out of the house by the back door?

"No, she is dead," they said.

But I did not understand. My daughter. So full of life? *Dead?* They must be wrong. I remember saying over and over again "That does not happen. That does not happen."

They brought out a chair for me to the pavement, and then brought out my daughter's dog which they had found cuddled, whimpering, next to her. I phoned her brother and sister. They and the friend arrived and then another friend who lived round the corner. My daughter had had a sudden haemorrhage from a gastric ulcer. She had cancelled the needed operation because COVID-19 was just then hitting the hospitals hard, and she had not wanted, in her lowered state of health, to go into one. She must have died the moment she looked out of the window, and fallen back, dead.

The police came – they have to attend the scene of any unexplained death. Senior Constable Nick Maguire and Constable Katerina Myskova (I name all of them because they were *people*, kind, sad and sorry; not just present in the line of duty) were called and then Phil

Mastoe and Emma Coffey arrived from The St John's Ambulance division that transports bodies for the Coroner's Court.

We were all out on the pavement, shaking with shock and horror. Suddenly, approaching down the road came a young woman holding a wobbling, half-size black-and-white Carnivale-style articulated skeleton. We all twelve of us stared. None of us knew whether to laugh or cry. So all of us, including the police, did both. Crying and laughing at this incredible, extraordinary sight at this dreadful, shocking time.

Then the Coroner's staff asked us to go for a short walk. Ten minutes they said. Why? So we would not be upset by witnessing her body being taken from her house.

"I was there the day Henrietta was born," I said. "So I will be there for her this day, the day she died." We stayed.

Out came a neat, covered gurney. It was loaded carefully into a white van with no markings. I am glad we stayed. And mourned. We witnessed the kindness and respect with which she was treated. If anything can be of comfort, that was.

I have written about this because, should this ever happen to you, I would like you to know how extraordinarily respectful, kind, and polite all these people were. The Ambos... the Police... the Coroner's men...

EIGHT MONTHS LATER

My son had been feeling unwell. Two biopsies just before Christmas, two blood tests just after. His wife had taken the children to the beach so he could sleep and feel better. I went round one evening to see him. He was cheery, funny, optimistic as usual. He had fainted several times during the day, but he was seeing his doctor at 8am the next morning, so all was under control, he said. Thinking that sleep was the best thing for him, I left.

The next day, I rang to see what the doctor had said. No answer. I went round. Found him.

Dead on the floor, looking peaceful, asleep.

The shock will never leave me. I am only thankful that his wife and small boys had not been the ones to walk in.

Again, my remaining daughter and I waiting outside in the drizzling rain as the Ambulance, then the Police then the Coroner's men combed the house and consulted in the street seemingly for hours and hours.

Standing while a second of my children was carried out of his house on a gurney.

Coroner's reports: It is important to understand that you may not receive a Coroner's report for six-seven months after a death. When you do, it will arrive in the post with a warning written on it: *not to open or read when you are alone as the contents can be distressing.* Believe that!

My son's report was thirty-seven pages long. We sat for an hour and a half with his GP trying to make head or tail of the medicalese. Rollo's health had been more complex that we had known (and maybe that he had understood) but if he had been taken to hospital that night he would not have died. A bitter, bitter thought.

DEATH, GRIEF & STARTING AGAIN

Living with the Shock

All deaths are different.

I thought those two days would be the worst of my life. But there was a third, equally as dreadful, to come.

We had not buried Henrietta's ashes as her other brother, Rodney, stranded by COVID-19 in London, had asked us to wait until he could be with us. Miraculously, he had managed to come. So we were able to bury their ashes together. Two of my children, aged 49 and 41. They, who had loved each other so much that she had gladly given him one of her kidneys, were now together, forever.

I was handed a spade of earth. I could not bury them. They were, and still are, not dead to me. They seem to be *alive* in my life even if they are not alive in this world.

About three weeks after that, a strange thing happened. I had been in intense distress, not surprisingly. I went for a walk on a beach with Henrietta's dog. The sun was beginning to set. The tide was coming in. A sudden wave hit the dog. Childbirth, plague, war, accident, old age, shipwreck. From the beginning of time, however, death comes to us the tide goes in, the tide goes out. The sun rises and the sun sets. Unknowing, uncaring.

A sudden feeling, a certainty swept over me, just as it had after my husband had died, that there was only one thing that I could, and must do for those around me, and that was not to be a problem to them. My family felt distraught, devastated, abandoned, in so many different ways. I knew I needed to look as if I coped, fed, exercised, cared for myself so that I would not be another load among the ones we all carried.

I walked off that beach with my wet dog, stronger than I had walked on to it.

Death is complicated. When my husband died, I had the comfort of knowing I had done everything I could for him. But these? These two adult children? A successful milestone with my daughter's business

– she had been working with great excitement on her new website the very day before she died. The *rage* that she had not taken the necessary steps to make sure she was still here, thrilled, to celebrate. I felt defeated. What more could I have done? Both had been so looking forward to the future – confident, successful, admired. Should I have interfered more than I had? Made them attend more to their health? The small boy blowing out the candles on his 7th birthday in tears because *Daddy was not there*. The three-year-old: "When is Daddy coming back?" I was filled with *rage*, watching.

Rollo had adored and, I suspect, had modelled himself upon his uncomplaining, stalwart grandfather. But that does not help if you need a hospital. All the regrets, all the questions. Should I have seen how ill he was that night? Thinking that he needed a sleep when he had just six hours to live when I left him? To *sleep*, as I thought, not to *die*. I know that I give the appearance of coping, but sometimes I think one can cope with grief more than one can cope with *shock*. Both these deaths were unforeseen, unexpected. Did that make them easier to bear than to watch someone's life trickling away in a hospital bed? Or suicide? I imagine that might be even worse.

I felt ill for months. Was it the understandable shock? Was old age suddenly creeping up on me? Or an undiagnosed horror waiting to be found? Many people find comfort in obtaining a diagnosis of depression. We are all different, but I have seen that when people are diagnosed with depression it can come as a relief – "Is *that* why I feel so bad?" Yet others feel that such a diagnosis defines yet one more problem to deal with on top of all the others facing them at that moment.

I noticed that every gentle phone call, every small kindness, thoughtful empathy, left me feeling I was not alone. My gloom was recognised. Hopefully as time goes on, small shards of comfort will grow.

I walked past our church. There is a small Garden of Remembrance. My two children lie there, buried together next to their father. I was overcome by a wave of absolute nausea. I have no acceptance, yet, but hopefully, one day that day will come.

I am OK if I keep busy. When I sit, idle, I feel them both beside me. Are they checking I am OK? Are they waiting for me to join them? Are they telling me they are happy? I wish I knew.

You do not get over such happenings in life... if you are lucky you manage to live *with* them. They do not go away.

Dear Ben,

I write this to you because perhaps you lost more than anyone else in this book.

At fifteen with some skylarking friends, you were thrown from a car and became quadriplegic. I know you had black moments of despair.

But if anyone is gloomy, I wish they could meet you. You are kind and funny, you are thoughtful and wise.

You told me that you still remember the tears in the eyes of your physiotherapist when, shortly after the accident, you told her that you would give yourself ten years, and if you still felt as you did then – that you would commit suicide. Five years later, you got your car licence and... you have never looked back. You told me that you felt it is important to give yourself *time* at such a moment in your life. You said that you now feel your life has amounted to much more because of your accident than if you had gone on being the heedless 15-year-old you were then. But you now realised the terrible toll it had taken on your family; that they had put all their efforts into helping you and you felt your brothers and sisters had suffered too.

Your father enrolled you in a New York Future Traders course, shortly after the accident, and you make a good living by playing the New York Options market. All you need for that is you, your cleverness and your computer. Your car is adapted, and your tractor specially designed with a hoist and a joystick so you can drive it and you work hard looking after the cows you love.

You have a glorious wife, and you love your two small children. Your horse came in last at the races. When asked what you were going to do you said with a slow smile, "I think I'll go home and beat up the wife" – you, who loved her and wouldn't... and *couldn't*... move a finger to hurt her. There was a silence and then a collapse of laughter, you laughing harder than all of us.

I know your life is hard, but I have learnt more from you than you can know, about what is hard and what is REALLY HARD.

And you made me think about what is sad and what is *really* sad.

You must have had blacker despair and deeper griefs than anyone else I know. If I find my life is hard, I think of yours and I know it is not. You are the most un-bitter person I know. You are loved by everyone who meets you. Including me.

Treasure yourself.

Love,
Diana

ACKNOWLEDGMENTS

I was overwhelmed at the deep level of care and commitment in every professional I talked to, and the love and care of those who told me told me their stories.

Some of you, kind friends, read the manuscript and made helpful suggestions. Others helped me find information that was hard to find – thank you!

Among many others: Deborah Bartlett-Pitt and Hugh Becker, Prof. Sue Beeton PhD, Alix Bradfield, Terence Bogue, Jane Clark, Liz Cunningham, Virginia Dahlenburg, Bin Dixon-Ward PhD, Joy Freier, Cornelia Goode, Alexandra Grimwade, Chloe Fitzwilliams-Hyde, Sarah Guest, Susie Hamson, Anne Latreille, Susie Lewis, Susan Morgan, Stan Pettigrew, Alan Preston, June Sherwood, Jenny Smith, Rosemary Syme, Logan Thurairatnam.

The Rt Rev Dr Peter Hollingworth AC OBE.

Rev Canon Dr Stephen Ames.

Georgina Barraclough, Registered nurse, Palliative Care/Complex Care/Rehabilitation.

Andrea Coote, Chair of the Aged Care Quality Advisory Council.

Nigel Davies BE MA GCBA. Funeral Director, Lonergan and Raven.

Mrs Joy Freier.

Kenneth Sheppard, Case Manager, Campbell Page.

Janice Tully BA Civil Celebrant.

Ben Sherer: thank you.

Simone Sherer, Certified Critical Care Nurse.

Vicki Steggal, Historian, Author.

Robin Syme, Michel Reymond and Robin Hunt for checking the legal pages.

Particular thanks to Lachlan Vallance – Principal, Accredited Specialist – Wills & Estates, Hicks, Oakley, Chessel, Williams, Lawyers & Notary.

USEFUL RESOURCES

Websites

The internet will connect you with services available in your own community, but it can be fascinating to read international, different approaches to a problem that faces us all, wherever we live. The United States is particularly sophisticated, the United Kingdom absorbing. Some services may be particular to your shire/council or suburb. Use these suggestions as a guide as to what may be available near you. Many of the following sites have been spoken of with admiration in my part of the world – I hope your part of the world is so lucky!

Ageing By Design Legal Advice
All subjects, legal, accommodation options: annacameron
@ageingbydesign.com.au

stephaniereeves@ageingbydesign.com.au

www.myagedcare.com.au basic, good, independent advice

Aged Care Quality Advisory Council
www.aacqa.gov.au

Living Longer Living Better – 2013 Reforms to Aged Care:
www.humanservices.gov.au
assesses aged-care needs and helps towards means-tested assistance to live longer in your own home

www.seniorsonline.vic.gov.au/seniors
help with seniors' loneliness Senior Citizens Centres et al

Aged Care Complaints Scheme **1800 550 552** anyone can raise a concern: partners, family, friends staff and volunteers

National Aged Care Advocacy Line **1800 700 600**
support during a complaints process

Information about aged care **1800 200 422**

Office of the Public Advocate: Independent advice on Elder Abuse, disabled children, Powers of Attorney et al.
www.publicadvocate.vic.gov.au
Emergency help: **1300 309 337**

www.humanservices.gov.au
if you care full-time for someone you may qualify
for a carers payment

www.seniorsrights.org.au
deals with elder abuse and support systems

www.agedcarecomplaints.govspace.gov.au
if you are deaf or have speech impairment call **1800 555 677**
and ask for **1800 550 552** for an interpreter **131 450**

DEPRESSION, ANXIETY SUPPORT

www.beyondblue.org.au
provides support for those suffering grief, anxiety or depression

www.griefline.org.au 1300 845 745

www.mariecurie.org.uk
good advice on facing and talking about death

www.rtssv.org.au
support for those who have suffered from road trauma

www.grief.org.au/ACGB/Publications/Resources
there is help here on many subjects: suicide, bushfire losses,
how to be a compassionate employer – returning to work

www.farmerhealth.org.au

www.mensshed.net

www.dullmensclub.com

SUICIDE

www.health.harvard.edu/newsletter_article/supporting-survivors-of-suicide-loss

www.survivorsofsuicide.com – good support provided

www.theaca.net.au
for deep-seated depression

www.humanservices.gov.au
provides links to a great variety of support systems

www.grief.org.au/ACGB/Publications/Resources

ROAD TRAUMA SUPPORT SERVICES

www.rtssv.org.au if you need support after road trauma

HEALTH SUPPORT

www.cancervic.org.au
Cancer Council Victoria – check out other people's stories

www.pallcarevic.com.au
Palliative Care Victoria

www.carergateway.gov.au

www.scopeaust.org.au

www.vmch.com.au

www.humanservices.gov.au/customer/service/centrelink/carer-allowance

www.betterhealth.vic.gov.au/supercarepharmacies – 24-hour pharmacy support and free out of hours advice

DEMENTIA

There is good support available:
the National Dementia Helplin **1800 699 799**

www.fightdementia.org.au

www.dementia.org.au good help in many languages

www.parliament.vic.gov.au>committees>Issues
informative inquiry into End of Life Choices

FUNERALS, COFFINS

www.gatheredhere.com.au
to compare prices in your area

info@albininternational.com
UK/international funerals

www.janetkeen.blogspot.com
make your own coffins

www.northwoodscasket.com
instructions on making a coffin

www.thecorpseproject.net
round the World/Los Catacumbas De Los Capucinos (Palermo) is a strikingly beautiful, riveting small film about the Palermo catacombs

LEGAL, MONEY, DIGITAL LIFE

www.hocw.com.au
Hicks, Oakley, Chessel, Williams:
good legal information and very useful checklist

www.statetrustees.com.au
information about the duties of an executor

www.publicadvocate.vic.gov.au
useful site, includes trust your choice, guides to choosing an executor

www.awayforabit.com
useful after-a death, advice for legacy, Facebook, managing your digital life etc., storing passwords

https://support.google.com
Google Inactive Account Manager

DIVORCE

www.moneysmart.gov.au/life-events-and-you/life-events/divorce-and-separation/divorce-and-separation-financial

http://www.australia.gov.au/information-and-services/family-and-community/realationships/getting-divorced

www.familycourt.gov.au
family breakup, mental health support

www.familyrelationships.gov.au

www.mindhealthconnect.org.au
their opening section is good

Books and other useful resources

Aisbett, Bev. *Taming the Black Dog*, Harper Collins – guide to overcoming depression – approachable, cartoon format, amusing to read. Pymble, 2000. Also All of It by Aisbett, Bev

Bolte-Taylor. *Jill My Stroke of Insight*, A Brain Scientist's Personal Journey Penguin Group 2006

Clark, Sally. *How to die happy – a practical handbook to make things easier for family and friends*, The best $12.95 you can spend. Comprehensive check-list type advice **www.howtodiehappy.com.au**

Mellonie, Brian and Ingpen, Robert. *Beginnings and Endings with Lifetimes in Between*, Penguin Random House 1983 – a particularly good book for small children

Doka, Dr Kenneth. *Grief is a Journey* Atria Books 2016

Hillman, Ken. *A Good Life to the End*, Taking control of our inevitable journey through aging and death Allen & Unwin 2017

Gawande, Atul. *Being Mortal*, Compassionate, thought provoking Metropolitan Books 2014

Kalanithi, Paul. *When Breath Becomes Air – What makes Life worth Living in the Face of Death*? A young neurosurgeon faces a terminal diagnosis Vintage 2016

Hitchcock, Karen. *Dear Life – on Caring for the Elderly* Quarterly Essay March 2015 a compassionate exploration of caring for those at the end-of-life

Hooker, Jeremy. *Diary of a Stroke* Shearsman Books 2010

Jordan, Kathleen with Steggal, Vicki. *My Story of Hope, Advocacy & Survival after Stroke* (a very good account of recovery after a stroke) Impact Press 2016

Kasket, Dr Elaine. *All the Ghosts in the Machine: Illusions of Immortality in the Digital Age* – dealing with digital legacies
Little Brown 2019

Lane, Rachel and Whittaker, Noel. *Aged care – who cares? where? how? & how much?* Informative, detailed exploration of nursing homes – cost-structure of various types of accommodation, etc. **www.agedcarewhocaresw.com.au**

Munro, Leah The Do-it-Yourself Funeral Book
lmunro@dodo.com.au

O'Mahony, Seamus. *The Way we Die Now deals with the depersonalisation and medicalisation of death.*
Head of Zeus UK 2016

Sampson, Fay. *Prayers for Dementia: And how to live well with it.*
Also: *Prayers for Depression: And how best to live with it*

Two books written from experience, both laced with compassion. Each deals with the person with the condition and also their family and wider community. Dartington, Longman,& Todd

Sandberg, Sheryl and Grant, Adam. *Option B: Facing Adversity, Building Resilience, and Finding Joy by Standing Up!*
Penguin Random House 2017

Winch, Sarah. *The Best Death – how to die well*
How to face death after a diagnosis, a sound, compassionate guide University of Queensland Press 2017

ABOUT THE AUTHOR

Diana Morgan AM, suffered the loss of a loving husband and two of her four adult children which is when she began to write this book.

Diana lives in Melbourne, Australia. She has had a long interest in the Arts, which has led to her being appointed a Member of the International Council of the Musée des Arts décoratifs, Paris since 1999. For fifteen years she was a member of the Coucil of The Australiana Fund, which looks after the Official Resdiences of the Governor and the Prime Minister of Australia. She is a Life Member of the National Gallery of Victoria and an ex-President of the National Gallery Women's Association.

Interested in living with the climate she wrote 'Succulents for Mediterranean Climate Gardens' in 2004 (Rosenberg).

Diana is about to publish a book on the History of Culinary Moulds.

If you have any corrections or additions
I would be glad to hear them.
Email: dianamarymorgan@protonmail.com

www.ingramcontent.com/pod-product-compliance
Lightning Source LLC
Chambersburg PA
CBHW030256010526
44107CB00053B/1732